Just Watch Me!

Trudeau's Tragic Legacy

by
Ron Coleman, Colonel (retired)

© Copyright 2003 R. D. Coleman. All rights reserved.

No part of this publication may be reproduced, stored in a retrieval system, or transmitted, in any form or by any means, electronic, mechanical, photocopying, recording, or otherwise, without the written prior permission of the author. Contact the author at rlcoleman@falls.igs.net or fax 613-283-4117.

Printed in Victoria, Canada

Cover and book designer: Fiona Raven
Front cover drawing: Irma Coucill / CP Picture Archive
Back cover photograph: Tom Hanson / CP Picture Archive

```
National Library of Canada Cataloguing in Publication Data

Coleman, R. D., 1945-
     Just watch me : Trudeau's tragic legacy / R.D.
Coleman.
Includes bibliographical references.
ISBN 1-55395-565-X
1. Canada—Politics and government—1993-   2. Trudeau, Pierre
2. Elliott, 1919-2000—Influence.  I. Title.
FC625.C64 2003          320.971'09'049      C2003-900158-X
F1034.2.C64 2003
```

TRAFFORD

This book was published *on-demand* in cooperation with Trafford Publishing. On-demand publishing is a unique process and service of making a book available for retail sale to the public taking advantage of on-demand manufacturing and Internet marketing. **On-demand publishing** includes promotions, retail sales, manufacturing, order fulfilment, accounting and collecting royalties on behalf of the author.

Suite 6E, 2333 Government St., Victoria, B.C. V8T 4P4, CANADA
Phone   250-383-6864   Toll-free   1-888-232-4444 (Canada & US)
Fax   250-383-6804   E-mail   sales@trafford.com
Web site www.trafford.com   TRAFFORD PUBLISHING IS A DIVISION OF TRAFFORD
HOLDINGS LTD.
Trafford Catalogue #02-1281   www.trafford.com/robots/02-1281.html

10   9   8   7   6   5   4   3   2

Contents

Introduction	v
1. Trudeau's Politics and Early Writings	1
2. He Came – He Saw – He Recreates	8
3. Trudeau Takes over Ottawa	15
4. Centralization	27
5. Socialism and Freedom are Mutually Exclusive	39
6. Principles and Ethics	46
7. Truth and Trudeau	58
8. Morals	64
9. Trading	70
10. Exert Prowess	77
11. Be Obedient and Disciplined	79
12. Tradition	81
13. Respect Hierarchy	83
14. Loyalty	87
15. Vengeance	89
16. Trudeau/Levesque Conspiracy – Deception	91
17. Leisure	98
18. Ostentatious	100
19. Largess	102
20. Exclusive	106
21. Fortitude	107
22. Fatalistic	110
23. Honour	112
24. Ideals	114
25. Elite	116
26. The Sun King	119
27. The Socialists Within	124
28. Economics	129
29. Legitimacy	135
30. So What do We do Now?	142
Bibliography	157

Dedicated

*to my wife, Linda
who inspires me
and to my sons, Rob and Jeff
who make me proud*

Acknowledgements

I wish to acknowledge the support I have received from my wife throughout this project. My friend and political advisor *Don Fowler* who was generous with advice and resources, suggested the title, was a great help and kept me going at times. I also want to thank *Joan Cochrane*, librarian, of the South Elmsley Branch of the Rideau Lakes Library system for her considerable help and assistance while I was researching and writing this book.

Although I loath labels, I have used terms like Francophone and Anglophone as well as others throughout because they have crept into the bureaucratic jargon. Despite the negative overtones they may illicit, in some, that was not my intent.

Introduction

Don't part with your illusions.
When they are gone you may still exist
but you have ceased to live.

– Mark Twain

Back in 1968, when I was much younger, I was so disillusioned with the perpetual Pearson/Diefenbaker debacle that I acted on compulsion without knowing much about Trudeau and placed my X beside the liberal in my riding. I have always regretted that and as penance will attempt to perhaps expose some of the damage that he and his erstwhile mimic Chrétien have done to Canada and Canadians. The tragedy that I intend to portray is not about Trudeau as much as it is about Canada. His was not a tragic life for he enjoyed privilege from birth to death. Canada however, has suffered internally and externally as the result of his perceived need to recreate Canada in his image. In short, he tried to play God but forgot that there is good and evil always at work against one another, in each of us, and it is often difficult to decide which is which. Trudeau put his plan into action and Canada came out the loser. Yet those in his party have persisted in following his blue print despite the mounting evidence that his vision of "social justice" was impaired. With his passing we continue to seek ways to right the wrongs he initiated, without wronging him.

Although employing the term liberal, the liberal party in Canada is in fact a socialist one and is leading Canada down the failure road that other countries have demonstrated too well to the detriment of their citizens. Borrowing on some often quoted terms, it is clear that liberals believe politically in pragmatism as opposed to principle and further embrace the view that citizens are here to serve the state rather than vice versa. Economically, they believe in state planning and control over competition. They prefer a mixed economy so that the benefits of wealth creation produced by capitalism can be transferred to their socialist intentions. To them truth is silly putty and they are the purveyors of continuous and biased propaganda. As Ayn Rand has stated: "The proper functions of a government fall into three broad categories, all of them involving the issues of physical force and the protection of men's rights: the police, to protect men from criminals—the armed services, to protect men from foreign invaders—the law courts, to settle disputes among men according to objective laws."[1] The job of governments then is to protect man's individual rights. It is in the unfettered pursuit of freedom under democracy and the free market that wealth is created which elevates all of the citizens of a country. In short, when men and women succeed economically the tide raises for all of us. Government interference in most of its forms, excepting real public goods, brings us all down. Our standard of living in Canada has progressively decreased since Trudeau came to power and similarly our influence in the "global village" has progressively diminished. Canada has a dismal record in the last 30 years in the pursuit of individual freedom. On the other hand, our progress towards a socialist state proceeds unabated. Much of this is the result of government interference in the market place and coercion of its citizens to participate in state programs, a practice that goes totally against individual freedom. Most of the problems faced by Canada today are the result of two socialist Prime Ministers, Lester Pearson and Pierre Trudeau.

    Much of what they and their followers have done in Canada is reversible but it will take time and it will be an uphill fight. This is because the Canadian people have fallen into a kind of funk that will resist the strongest medicines that must be brought to bear. Our economy remains dependant on the U.S. as does our dollar although now it is hardly that. Our political institutions are moribund or downright irrelevant. The elites control the country and every special interest receives goodies from the governments. Our different levels of government are in constant conflict and our federal, and I suspect, provincial and municipal public servants are uncommitted to the people they serve. Internationally, we have relegated our sovereignty to the United Nations and have given only lip service to collective security. We have reached and surpassed the tax levels that persecute initiative and hard work. We are losing our best and brightest, often trained at our expense, to other nations, mostly the U.S. because they find more satisfaction, challenge, entrepreneurship, interest, fulfillment, and less obstruction/difficulty in pursuing ideas there. Our leaders deny this reality and thus see no need to address it. Our totally open and porous immigration policy combined with our multiculturalism approach has introduced considerable strife to this country that was not there even 30 years ago. By assisting other cultures to come here and maintain their values and beliefs instead of attempting to adopt ours we are essentially importing the stresses and strains of those who have immigrated in order to put these problems behind them. It then becomes harder for us to know what Canadians are and stand for. To this point in our history, and we are still a young country, we still attempt to define ourselves by what we are not rather than what we are. Continued unfiltered immigration will only aggravate this already ambiguous national psyche. Canada seems to be a nation of myths and governs accordingly. It is well known, by any scholar, that Canada has at least two histories, English and French. Both are heavily biased and therefore suspect and they are vastly different.

For example, Louis Riel is both a hero and a villain at the same time. The fact that we have never really been able or willing to get this fundamental of our society right has caused us to run parallel concepts of the truth in our education systems and in other social areas as well. That our citizens are confused and hostile and easily put on one side or the other is easy to contemplate. Politicians, like Trudeau, have used this fissure to fracture rather than fuse us. If we do not soon wake up and come together as a nation we will be taken over willingly and bloodlessly by our southern neighbour, who already controls us economically. Moreover, we will not deserve to persist. I do not think our prospects are good but I am hopeful. The solution is to select people with the right character to represent us in government and to return our Parliament to an effective institution of the people.

An institution that functions on principles that can answer yes to the following: "Is man a sovereign individual who owns his person, his mind, his life, his work and its products—or is he the property of the tribe (the state, the society, the collective) that may dispose of him in any way it pleases, that may dictate his convictions, prescribe the course of his life, control his work and expropriate his products? Does man have the right to exist for his own sake—or is he born in bondage, as an indentured servant who must keep buying his life by serving the tribe but can never acquire it free and clear?"[2] Simply, is man free? In this book we will look at Trudeau and his policies from this perspective and you will see that Canadians were not and are not.

End Notes

1. Ayn Rand, *"Capitalism: The Unknown Ideal,"* New York, The New American Library, 1946, p. 300.
2. Ibid., p. 11.

1

Trudeau's Politics and Early Writings

David Somerville has captured the character and beliefs of Trudeau by examining his writings and interviewing Trudeau's friends and compatriots throughout his life, both public and private. Somerville has demonstrated in my view, without stating it, that Trudeau was a socialist, a pacifist, anti-military and a communist sympathizer. He was profoundly anti-American and heavily influenced by socialist and communist writers. In his book, *"Trudeau Revealed: By His Actions and Words"*, Somerville has helped to solve the enigma that was Trudeau. There was plenty of material to reveal who Trudeau was and what he stood for but unfortunately none or little of it was available to most Canadians outside Quebec before he came to power. Even today many Canadians are unaware of how this Prime Minister fundamentally changed federal politics and why. I believe the following quotes from Trudeau's friends found in the book will serve to expose the real Trudeau.

Jean de Grandpre, a classmate of Trudeau at the elite Jesuit classical college, Jean de Brebeuf, said he displayed "a certain arrogance which even then led him to ridicule people who were not too bright" and that he was "a dilettante ... spoiled brat ... intellectual snob and lone wolf".[1]

When war broke out Trudeau joined the Canadian Officer' Training Corps as required in his final year at Brebeuf. Trudeau was remembered as a poor soldier who was more interested in pranks and usurping authority than learning. In 1942 he actively participated in the League for the Defence of Canada which formed in order to combat conscription.

He later studied at Harvard and was heavily influenced by Professor Joseph Schumpeter who published a book entitled, "Capitalism, Socialism and Democracy", in which he described the emergence of socialism from the failure of capitalism. He then went to study at the Sorbonne in France and while there met a French activist, Emmanuel Mounier, who was the founder of "Esprit", a catholic review with a leftist view. This was no doubt the inspiration for Trudeau and Pellitier when they founded Cité Libre later in Quebec. Mounier believed that Communism was the right political system for France but he was opposed to violence as a means to achieve it as had been the case in other countries. Years later Trudeau acknowledged the influence Mounier had on him in his youth.

Trudeau left Paris for London where he studied under the direct tutelage of Professor Harold Laski, of the London School of Economics. Laski, was a socialist whose teachings were in part as follows:

"The necessarily federal character of society; the incompatibility of the sovereign state with that economic world order so painfully struggling to be born; the antithesis between individual property rights in the essential means of production and the fulfilment of the democratic idea; the thesis that liberty is a concept devoid of real meaning except in the context of equality...

"There cannot, in a word, be democracy unless there is socialism..."[2]

After his formal education was complete Trudeau set out on his travels to East Europe, the Middle East, the Far

East and China. Upon his return to Canada, and Montreal, he began a period of activism along with his friends and old school mates. One of them, Jean-Louis Gagnon, who had left the Labour Progressive Party, (Communist), for the Liberals described Trudeau at this time: "Pierre was not a Liberal, he was quite a radical. He was fresh out of the London School of Economics and a Fabian socialist."[3] He took a job in Ottawa in the Privy Council Office but spent most of his week ends in Montreal where along with his associates they decided to set up Cite Libre. This became Trudeau's vehicle for challenging Duplessis, Quebecers, Catholics, America, and anyone else who did not share his views for the next few years. He left the PCO in 1951 and during a trip to Europe took a side trip to Moscow to attend a world economic conference hosted by the Soviet Union. It is not clear just how Trudeau was invited to attend and became part of the Canadian delegation. According to his fellow Canadian delegates Trudeau contributed little and spent much of his time gallivanting around Moscow. Trudeau however, described his fellow delegates as "lightweights". After the conference Trudeau stayed in the USSR and toured for another two weeks before he was pointedly asked to leave, according to him.

Upon return to Canada he wrote extensively about the conference and the Soviet system and it appeared that most of what he had to say was supportive of the Soviet system. It stirred up criticism and resulted in traded insults in the press between Trudeau and his adversaries. He was attacked by a Father Braun and later by the editor of Nos Cours, a religious review, Reverend J. B. Desrosiers: "While it's true that Mr. Trudeau mentioned inequalities, planned famines, counter-revolutions and the suppression of millions of 'Kulaks,' the balance of his series leans all too noticeably toward admiration and apology for a system which is choking the people …"[4]

Trudeau's first reference to bilingualism appears in 1954

when he agreed with Duplessis in a federal-provincial confrontation. Rather than return a $2 million subsidy to its universities from the federal government he suggested that Duplessis accept the subsidy and channel it into separate schools, bonuses to federal civil servants and make bilingual plaques for federal buildings, embassies and federal transport. "This policy would serve three ends, said Trudeau. It would underline Duplessis' opposition to federal meddling, prevent two million dollars being returned to the federal government for its use and "furnish precious aid to the French Canadian culture".[5] It is interesting that later as PM Trudeau would continually meddle in Provincial affairs, lavish federal money on Quebec and do everything he could to aid French Canadian culture.

At this point in his life Trudeau began to take political action while continuing to write. He and his associates decided to start a new political party, Le Rassemblement. Trudeau was made the vice-president. At this same time Trudeau became involved as the editor in a book of essays entitled, "The Asbestos Strike". As before, Trudeau was attacked publicly by those who disagreed with his views. A noted French Canadian historian, Robert Rumilly, wrote a book entitled, "The Leftist Infiltration of French Canada" that attacked the views of Trudeau and his friends: "In 147 pages of detailed documentation, Rumilly exposed what he believed was an insidious, well-managed network dedicated to socialism and the destruction of the authority of the Church and the State."[6] Rumilly went on to criticize the editors of several French dailies for giving Trudeau and his associates exposure and CBC's Radio-Canada for using taxpayers money to promote them and their views. For this and other reasons Trudeau and his associates were taking on certain notoriety.

Trudeau was now becoming known outside Quebec and in particular in Ottawa where the ruling Liberal party was looking for some fresh talent, especially French talent.

Despite the perceived betrayal by Pearson and the liberal party in their policy reversal on nuclear weapons, Trudeau, Marchand, and Pellitier were being wooed into joining the federal liberals. Notwithstanding Trudeau's stated abhorence of nuclear weapons, they were in storage for use in Canada throughout his reign. He did, however, eliminate them from the strike mission in Europe early in his first government. For Trudeau, the party of choice was not as important as being on the party that acquired power. This is a character flaw that many politicians have and many of them change parties willy nilly after entering politics. He believed he could be part of that with the Liberals who enjoyed support in Quebec. He wrote the following about his fellow French Canadians:

"Historically, French Canadians have not really believed in democracy for themselves ... "In all important aspects of national politics, guile, compromise, and a subtle kind of blackmail decided their course and determined their alliances. They appeared to discount all political or social ideologies, save nationalism..." French Canadians voted "only for the man or group which stood for their ethnic rights... Liberals "have always encouraged Quebecers to continue using their voting bloc as an instrument of racial defence, or of personal gain. Their only slogans have been racial slogans... 'Vote for a party led by a French Canadian'... and it was on the strength of such slogans that they were elected.[7]

Liberal ideology as Trudeau put it is that "we are a party of the radical centre."[8] More accurately, the liberal party is the party of pragmatism that will do anything to maintain power. William D. Gairdner points out in his excellent book, *"The Trouble With Canada"*, that the liberal party no longer stands for liberalism.

"Canada's modern liberal party has nothing to do with classical liberalism and its defence of the individual. In fact, like U.S. Democrats, the modern Liberal in Canada is much more strongly associated with the promotion of the State and all its powers than with defending the freedoms of the individual. This wholesale switch in the ideological position of liberals took a mere century to bring about and in Canada was vastly accelerated by Pierre Trudeau and his 'liberal' — especially French Canadian — colleges."[9]

This is an important point. Although it is often said that Canadians are pragmatists I do not share the view. I think Canadians are much more principled but that is not the case with politicians and political parties. This characteristic has been much more in evidence of late because of the proliferation of Canadians from Quebec in federal politics, especially as leaders. If we look back into the cultures of the English and the French we can note this is historically sound reasoning. We also see it in the type of ideology that has evolved in England and France. In the former we see democracy and in the latter we see socialism.

Trudeau was not reluctant to adopt and claim policies and plans from other parties throughout his terms of office. On "balance", another common word used by Trudeau and subsequent liberal governments, was that he plied the middle ground however, the middle ground was socialist ground as by the time he rose to power Pearson had taken many of the first steps in creating a welfare state. Based on President Johnson's "Great Society Programs" in the U.S., Pearson sought to emulate them. LBJ and the American people abandoned most of these plans because they could not afford them but Canada pressed on to the detriment of the Treasury. So although Trudeau held to the middle ground it had shifted well to the political left and he would take it further. You will remember that these were the heady days of the NDP and the liberals used the New Democratic Party (NDP) well in order to retain control. David Lewis and his hapless party were willing victims and although they thought at the time that they would win favour with the public for their open liberal support, history has proven them wrong. They continue to reap the rewards of co-conspirators.

The situation we find ourselves in today is one which Trudeau described and forewarned about in *"The Essential Trudeau"*. "Ideological systems are the true enemies of freedom. On the political front, accepted opinions are not only inhibiting to the mind, they contain the very source of error. When a political ideology is universally accepted by the elite, when the people who "define situation" embrace and venerate it, this means that it is high time free men were fighting it. For political freedom finds its essential strength in the sense of balance and proportion. As soon as any one tendency becomes too strong, it constitutes a menace."[10] I think the media and some of the liberal spin doctors could learn from this and certainly the Canadian people who continue to mortgage their heirs' standard of living and their own to the tax and spend policies of the socialists in Ottawa.

End Notes

1. David Somerville, *"Trudeau Revealed: By His Actions and Words,"* BMG Publishing Ltd., Richmond Hill, 1978, pp. 6–7.
2. Ibid., p. 196.
3. Ibid., p. 39.
4. Ibid., p. 66.
5. Ibid., p. 87.
6. Ibid., p. 100.
7. Ibid., pp. 122–123.
8. Pierre Trudeau, *"The Essential Trudeau,"* McLelland and Stewart, Toronto, 1998, p. 71.
9. William Gairdner, *"The Trouble With Canada,"* General Paperbacks, Toronto, 1991, p. 1
10. Pierre Trudeau, *"The Essential Trudeau,"* McLelland and Stewart, Toronto, 1998, pp. 6–7.

2

He Came — He Saw — He Recreates

Trudeau came to Ottawa with a mission that was rooted in his perceptions that Canada had wronged Quebec and he would set it straight. In *"The Essential Trudeau"* writing about Quebec Nationalism he states his views on the treatment of Quebec by the rest of Canada. "A people which had been defeated, occupied, decapitated, pushed out of commerce, driven from the cities, reduced little by little to a minority, and diminished in influence in a country which it had nonetheless discovered, explored, and colonized, could adopt few attitudes that would enable it to preserve its identity. This people devised a system of security, which became overdeveloped; thus as a result, it sometimes overvalued all those things that set it apart from others, and showed hostility to all change (even progress) coming from without."[1]

Again in *"The Essential Trudeau"* when discussing Canadian Patriotism, Trudeau demonstrates his perception of the history of English-French relations that shaped his view and his subsequent acts when he came to Ottawa. "Since the French Canadians had the bad grace to decline assimilation, such identification was beyond being completely realizable. So the Anglo-Canadians built themselves an illusion of it by fencing off the French

Canadians in their Quebec ghetto and then nibbling at its constitutional powers and carrying them off bit by bit to Ottawa. Outside Quebec they fought, with staggering ferocity, against anything that might intrude upon that illusion: the use of French on stamps, money, cheques, in the civil service, the railroads, and the whole works."[2] With these views firmly imprinted in his mind he set off to Ottawa to establish the "French Fact" in Canada.

Quoted by Ramsey Cook in "Towards a Just Society" in 1962 Trudeau wrote in *"La Nouvelle Trahison des clercs"*:

> The die is cast in Canada: there are two main ethnic and linguistic groups; each is too strongly and too deeply rooted in the past, too firmly bound to a mother culture, to be able to engulf the other. But if the two will collaborate at the hub of a truly pluralistic state, Canada will become the envied seat of a form of federalism that belongs to tomorrow's world. Better than the American melting pot, Canada could offer an example to all those new Asian and African states... who must discover how to govern their polyethnic populations with proper regard for justice and liberty. What better reason for cold-shouldering the lure of annexation to the United States?[3]

Despite the fact that Trudeau ignores the contribution to Canada's population from, our aboriginals, the United Empire Loyalists, (not the same as English) the millions of emigrants and their descendants from European countries other than France or England, our more recent additions from Asia, and those of us who consider ourselves Canadians first, this quote captures three themes that permeate Trudeau's governance. First, is the exclusion of all Canadians other than of English or French origin; second, is the rabid distaste for all things American; third, is the ethnocentric concept that other countries could learn from us, a view that was carried to extremes later by Lloyd Axworthy and Foreign Affairs in Chrétien's government.

The point here is that Trudeau's government was all about, and only about, Quebec and her place in Canada.

The significant fact is that Trudeau was wrong about the English wronging the French. The truth that belies this myth is contained in Trudeau's own words. The English ensured through the Quebec Act that Lower Canada would maintain her own language and legal system. The English did not maintain the Seigneur and Serf system, the French did. The English did not force the French to attend Catholic schools, the clergy did. The English did not make the church the focus of life in Quebec, the French did. The English did not restrict the French to an agricultural society. Other Canadians did not elect Premier Duplessi who was the focus of a young Trudeau and the target of his criticism. And last, the English did not persecute the French. So if you don't buy into the French projection of their backwardness until the quiet revolution, on the English, why must the English atone?

Yolanda East Cossette a Canadian from Quebec, in fact from the Lac-St.-Jean area, the heartland of separatism, who left Quebec early in life certainly does not share the view of English persecution. In her book, *"The Weak Link: Quebec"*, she makes this point strongly. "French Canadians have been encouraged, through the last two centuries, to resist any kind of co-operation with the English. They refused to adapt to the irrevocable reality, and instead chose to use the English as scapegoats to be blamed for all their ills."[4] She makes the point again later in the book:

> Religion kept those French Canadians down, not the English. Most traditional rural French Canadians have the mentality of third World Nations. Sexual obsession dominates their thinking, while they seem to have no thirst for knowledge, they are perfectly satisfied with third hand information. That makes them an easy people to manipulate.

A flock of sheep to follow the shepherd. Most of them are completely incapable of thinking for themselves. They just repeat slogans, or the pre-digested ideas in vogue. Fashion and the shallow pursuits of a superficial life dominated by the love of money, aptly describes most traditional French Canadians. Their ignorance is appalling! They have never been able to govern themselves. Religion has killed their social conscience, and encouraged masochistic behaviour. Paranoia is cultivated by the Government.[5]

Mrs. Cossette's views are very strong, partly because she is from Quebec originally and has now returned to live there. She left Quebec at the age of 19 and comments that upon arrival in Toronto, "My identity crisis was suddenly over; I simply couldn't go back to my French ghetto. I have been at odds with my family and my compatriots ever since."[6] Her views are expressed with conviction and she is definitely not a hyphenated Canadian stating clearly that: "with European roots, a Caucasian ancestry and a French-Canadian education. My home province is Quebec; I consider myself a Canadian first and a Quebecer second."[7]

A committed separatist, Dr. Marcel Chaput, an employee of the federal government, and president of the Rassemblement pour l'independence Nationale, stated his views on bilingualism and English persecution in, the book, *"Quebec States Her Case"*. "I cannot stand by silently, as others seemingly can, and watch the day-by-day extermination of my people, even if by our own foolishness we are more to blame than the 'damned English'.[8] Clearly, bilingualism is not something that Quebecers support strongly; in fact they see it as an effort to encapsulate their culture into the Canadian one. Also, he clearly does not blame the English for Quebec's cultural problems even though he demonstrates his hatred toward them. Nonetheless, here is a separatist willingly in the employ of the

Queen while actively participating against the Queen and country. Unfortunately, many of the beneficiaries of bilingualism and particularly biculturalism today share this view. It is the practised art and sentiment of treason.

Looking back we need to bear in mind that at the time of the Battle between Montcalm and Wolfe there were only about one million people in Canada, and more French than English. Now we have 33 million of which approximately 24% may believe the myth of English persecution of the French. In reality if the English had been successful conquerors the myth might have some credibility, but as in many other cases involving colonies of their fallen Empire they erred and facilitated the growth of two cultures in one country. They too ignored the natives as equals in the Dominion. Canadians need not feel guilt or atone for anything; and some Canadians should not feel that Canada somehow owes them.

It is the norm in politics to project blame for one's own shortcomings onto someone or something else. It is also a natural human fault that we have all practiced at one time or another. It is the favoured practice of children and politicians. Your child blames his sister or brother; the politician blames the other party or another country. If our dollar drops in value it is because of the money speculators not lack of productivity. If the economy tanks it is the fault of the U.S. etc. Why Canadians believe this nonsense is because they want to rather than face the fact that their problems are often home grown. Anyway, the concept that Trudeau thought English Canada somehow owed Quebec is flawed by his and his followers' narrow and pathetic view that Quebec has been wronged since 1759. It is time for Canadians who still harbour guilt to cast it off and place the responsibility where it belongs with the French themselves. Other Canadians owe them nothing. Trudeau hints at this very fact when he states that this people built themselves a system of security that fenced them in. Canadians need to change this skewed view of our history so that they aren't subjected in future to this kind of revisionist thinking or subtle blackmail. Moreover, when faced with it they should reject it for the nonsense it is.

It is for this misplaced guilt that Trudeau succeeded to the degree he did! But in order to do so he had to discard many of his own ideals. Writing in Cite Libre in April 1962, Trudeau commenting on the state of Quebec nationalism states that: "Any effort aimed at strengthening the nation must avoid dividing it."[9] Nonetheless that is exactly what bilingualism has done. He goes on to say: "A truly democratic government cannot be 'nationalist', because it must pursue the good of all its citizens, without prejudice to ethnic origin."[10] Again, biculturalism is precisely discrimination based on ethnic origin. He then goes on to ridicule and chastise Quebecers for their nationalistic views. "But the ultimate tragedy would be in not realizing that French Canada is too culturally anaemic, too economically destitute, too intellectually retarded, too spiritually ossified, to be able to survive more than a couple of decades of stagnation, emptying herself of all her vitality into nothing but a cesspit, the mirror of her nationalistic vanity and 'dignity'...." [11] Thus, he was setting up the means to exploit the paranoia and ill will of Quebecers and the generosity of the rest of Canada to achieve his end, the Frenchification of Canada. It is hard to escape the political expediency and the hypocrisy of Trudeau evidenced in his words. A house of cards built on a foundation of false premises is bound to collapse.

End Notes

1. Pierre Trudeau, *"The Essential Trudeau,"* McLelland and Stewart, Toronto, 1998, p. 108.
2. Ibid., p. 132.

3. Pierre Trudeau and Thomas Axworthy, "*Towards a Just Society*," Toronto: McLelland and Stewart Ltd., 1993, p. 6.
4. Yolanda Cossette, "*The Weak Link: Quebec*," Louisville: Imprimerie Gagne Ltee., 1989, p. 15.
5. Ibid., p. 35.
6. Ibid., p. 38.
7. Ibid., p. 38.
8. Frank Scott, "*Quebec States Her Case*," Toronto: Macmillan of Canada, 1964, p. 52.
9. Ibid., p. 62.
10. Ibid., p. 63.
11. Ibid., p. 64.

3

Trudeau Takes Over Ottawa

Richard Gwyn writes in wonder at how Trudeau came to power and how he captivated the hearts and minds of Canadians. In his book *"The Northern Magus"* he writes after four years of deliberating on the mystique of Trudeau: "Now I understand: he is a great magician."[1] Indeed, he was, and like all great magicians he was capable of great illusions. The foundation of his design on making permanent the French Fact in Canada was in the use of the Pearson Royal Commission on Bilingualism and Biculturalism (B&B). Anyone who has read this document would not take much exception to it but like all bad legislation the devil was in the details and Trudeau set about marketing his version of it to the great unwashed. In essence the B&B Commission did not recommend the kind of bilingualism foisted on Canada by Trudeau. They recommended a form of territorial bilingualism whereby economy and practicality would determine where linguistic help would be provided. Trudeau however, believed that everyone should be able to receive services in either official language regardless of location within Canada. This, of course, was a much bigger and difficult task and as we have seen much more divisive and expensive. As Scott Reid points out in his book, *"Lament for a*

Notion", what we finally wound up with was asymmetric bilingualism:

> The asymmetric view holds that in the nine provinces where French is a minority language, minorities should be shown every generosity, and their institutions liberally subsidized. The active goal of language policy outside Quebec should be to limit or halt assimilation into English. Within Quebec asymmetrical bilingualism calls for the adoption of whatever measures are necessary to ensure that French continues to grow as the language of an ever-larger proportion of the population. Because demographic trends would not make this happen on its won, asymmetrical bilingualism requires, at best, the bare toleration of Quebec's English-speaking minority.[2]

One wonders how such a policy could be perceived as assisting unity. It could only be divisive. Nevertheless, the party and bureaucracy proceeded at break neck pace and in every manner introduced residual legislation to implement B&B. The quicker it was done on a massive scale the less easily it would be to reverse. This was the tactical plan. Trudeau recruited the personnel he needed to "make it so". The myth that Trudeau created to justify his actions was the extension of the persecution myth combined with the proposed myth that by making the federal government reflect the national racial mix, minus all others except English and French, all would be well. Professor Hayek in his book, *"The Road to Serfdom"*, has this to say about myth making: "This process of creating a "myth" to justify his action need not be conscious. The totalitarian leader may be guided merely by an instinctive dislike of the state of things he has found and a desire to create a new hierarchical order which conforms better to his conception of merit; ... youth."[3] The other aspect of this myth was that Quebecers were not welcome in other parts of Canada and that if everyone was bilingual this would dissolve. There is neither substance nor proof that Quebecers were or are unwelcome in other parts of Canada. Certainly there are language barriers but that hasn't made anyone unwelcome. We welcome immigrants who do not speak English or French. Our indigenous citizens get along without knowing either. This was Trudeau's way of concocting a case to foist B&B on a tolerant and compassionate society. He abandoned logic, his moniker, and played on the emotions, a favourite ploy of politicians to stir the unsatisfied among us.

Although Trudeau is acclaimed as being the product of two systems he clearly preferred the French culture and political approach to the English. That there are significant differences in the two should not come as a surprise but they are quoted here from William Gairdner in his book, *"The Trouble with Canada"*:

> An easier way to conceive of the French style of government is simply as a top-down concept that exerts a broad control through elitism, government coercion, and social engineering, all of which are upheld by granting the State special rights to abrogate freedoms. (Canada's constitution grants the State this right.) The essence of this style lies in its willingness to design different rules for different social groups in the interests of engineering an equal result for all.
>
> Rooted in the ancient concept of "natural rights" and further developed in the eighteenth century by John Locke, the English style emphasises free will, individual responsibility for one's deeds, and political and economic freedom with all the contractual rights and legal protections attached thereto. Its dominant feature is not power, but liberty.[4]

In Canada a short look at history will demonstrate dramatically that we have shifted, quite quickly, from the latter style of government to the former and I am not convinced that the people of Canada are even aware of how deftly Trudeau and his confreres pulled it off. Nonetheless, the battle lines persist after centuries between these two opposed ideologies.

It did not take long, after Trudeau became PM, for Quebecers to take over the cabinet, the bureaucracy, and by extension Canada. This is explained by Trudeau writing on democracy in *"The Essential Trudeau"*: "For instance, democracy cannot be made to work in a country where a large part of the citizens are by status condemned to a perpetual state of domination, economic or otherwise. Essentially, a true democracy must permit the periodic transformation of political minorities into majorities."[5] This was the end and B&B was the means. Now all Trudeau had to do was disguise it as the "common good" and "social justice" and feed it to the guilty and gullible Anglophones. The details of B&B were either denied or obscured and if anyone was really opposed to the program they could be branded racist and the media would take care of them. Character assignation was and remains a favourite tactic against those who oppose socialism. It works in all socialist societies. Besides the "Trudeauites" controlled the Canadian Broadcasting Corporation (CBC). Combined with their own propaganda machine, the Prime Ministers Office (PMO), they were able to suppress resistance.

Even Trudeau was surprised by the ease and magnitude of the take-over. Writing in *"Towards a Just Society"* he quotes his friend: "Pelletier makes it clear that the Official Languages Act was no panacea— unilingualism, as he says, is alive and well — but through it we did achieve a transformation in the public service, and more importantly, there was an outpouring of goodwill and changed behaviour across Canada as hundreds of thousands of Canadians endorsed the ethic of bilingualism. In 1965, for example, francophones comprised 22 percent of the federal public service; by 1984 that percentage had increased to 28 percent, well above the percentage of them in the population as a whole (24 percent). Indeed, by 1988 they held 30.5 percent of officer positions in the national capital region (NCR) of Ottawa-Hull."[6] Another change made by Trudeau was to change the capital from Ottawa to Ottawa-Hull, another way to benefit Quebec by directing departments and taxpayer dollars across the Ottawa River.

Pelletier was mistaken. Silence does not equal approval and most Canadians follow their political leaders who in this case acquiesced even though they did not believe in Trudeau's bilingualism. In this case the opposition was disloyal to Canadians because they failed to oppose this policy. "There were some notes of protest from English Canada at the thought that someone would have to pay for all the new services and that bilingualism might become an imposition on the individual rather than on the state. But the opposition parties knew the mathematics of winning power, so they were silent, and voted in favour of the bill."[7] In any country there should be two overriding criteria when it comes to the striking of new laws. First, it should be good for all the citizens, not just some. And second, it should be good for the country, the whole country. If in either case it pits one group against another or one region against another then it should be rejected. Provincial governments are in place to handle regional legislation and municipalities for local ones. State-wide policies however should benefit all. This is where the Senate should come into play, as our forefathers intended, but as we are well aware it is now composed of party sell outs and rabid party loyalists.

B&B proceeded unimpeded and more and more francophones won the lottery. Since Trudeau the percentage has expanded under various Commissioners of Languages and the federal governments to today under

Jean Chrétien (JC). And there is no end to the ways in which the liberals strive to achieve and maintain francophones in a majority position within the public service. For example, the latest Commissioner wants to abolish the bilingual bonus and make bilingualism a prerequisite for employment with the federal public service. This would effectively make the entire federal bureaucracy French by origin. It would also eliminate those from other regions of Canada from work within the federal public service. In other words unilingual Anglophones need not apply. Ms. Adams argues that bilingualism has been enforced by rules and quotas over the years that breed resentment rather than an "understanding of the cultural and social values" of linguistic duality. On this last point I agree with her. There has been and is great resentment. What else would you expect from a program that has cost Canadians billions and benefited only a select group? Her proposals will only generate more hostility.

The *Ottawa Citizen*, 4 August, 2002, reports that jobs designated bilingual account for 37% of the 148,400 federal positions across Canada. The proportion is much higher in the NCR, where 63% of nearly 58,600 jobs are bilingual. Of course Ottawa is where most of the planning and policies are concocted therefore, the influence of francophones has already achieved Trudeau's envisioned majority. Also, these figures do not include the RCMP, Canadian Forces, and the countless government funded agencies, commissions, boards, etc., that are appointed by the PM and his minions. Canadians need to reflect on this "French Fact" the next time they go to the polls, especially those in Ontario who repeatedly guarantee the liberals victory. A victory they pay heavily for.

Today, in the summer of 2002 when parliament is in recess and the heat is upon us our intergovernmental affairs ministers chides the rest of the provinces for not following the example of New Brunswick and make themselves totally bilingual. Forget the fact that we are in a stock market meltdown and the world economy is on its butt. Forget the wasted billions already spent on translating documents that set unused on shelves. Forget that Trudeau and his liberals refused to challenge Bill 101 in Quebec even though it is patently unconstitutional and that Quebec remains unilingual French. The 1996 census revealed that with the exception of N.B. and Quebec no other province or territory has more than 4% French overall. Yet we are asked to provide bilingual services in them all. On the other hand, in Quebec there are 8% English who are denied English language rights. The Quebec government has invoked the infamous "notwithstanding" clause in Trudeau's Canadian Constitution in order to do so. Does this seem reasonable? And yet all federal governments since Trudeau have failed to challenge Quebec on this issue. It is a sorry credit to the rest of Canada that we have not risen up and demanded that this injustice/discrimination be reversed. Forget the fact that the whole world continues to use English more and more as the language of preference. Forget the fact that the PQ use monies from equalization to fund the language police and harass lawful citizens for sign infractions etc. Why not, we will all just forget reality and spend more billions on the socialist dream and Trudeau's goal. And we Canadians wonder why other countries don't take us too seriously.

There is however an explanation for why the feds have not challenged Bill 101. As Scott Reid points out in his book *"Lament for a Notion"* the Prime Minister attempted to buy back the loyalty of Quebecers with transfer payments believing this would make them see the error of Bill 101. He was mistaken. Although businesses and people fled Quebec the Quebec treasury did not suffer at all, in fact, it gained because as Quebec's per-capita income fell transfer payments were increased. "Quebec's per-capita GNP took a hosing as the province haemorrhaged Anglophones between 1977 and 1987, but during this period the province absorbed $23.6 billion in federal equalization payments (more than all Canada's other provinces combined)."[8] As Reid points out this made the PQ look like the saviours of the French language; through transfer payments Anglophones were in fact paying for unilingual French policy indirectly; the French benefited from the plunge in housing costs created by the English exodus; and the monies transferred had no strings attached therefore the PQ could direct them wherever they needed to support their programs. Trudeau had been outmanoeuvred by Jacques Parizeau, PQ finance minister at the time, but because of his inflated and enflamed ego he would not now challenge Bill 101. To date neither has any other leader of the federal government and the spending continues in Quebec at the expense of Ontario and Alberta citizens.

How could this flight to fancy have taken place? How could perfectly reasonable people allow a minority to assert itself to the extent where they commit billions to a bilingual program that was destined to fail? And one that Quebecers have no interest in. It happened because of the intelligent use of deception. Trudeau knew that the bilingual part of the program would draw fire and it did. That did not bother him because while the critics, media, and opposition railed at him he used the familiar tactic of socialists to invoke racism against those who opposed the program. Meanwhile biculturalism, the real injustice, was being implemented at a breakneck pace. I watched it myself while in the military. Beginning in the early 1970's, francophones were being promoted in droves and we wondered what was going on while our complicit and co-opted leadership denied that preferences were being made. Similarly, the same was happening in the RCMP and in the public service.

After a few years I was in the position of supervising as well and was aghast at how well the propaganda had worked. Anglophone junior officers and many senior ones truly believed that they were competing on a balanced field. They were at first confused, then gripped by denial, and finally by disappointment when I told them that there were 28% of all ranks in all classifications and trades that they could not compete for. Most of the people I supervised were pilots, not unintelligent individuals, but they had been completely duped by the government and their leaders. Many of them left the service after finding out the truth; I myself left the regular force when I could no longer support B&B, among other things. For me this was a sad ending to a good career and I am not complaining. It was just not fair and in good conscience I could not go on. I joined the Air Reserve instead where B&B was not an active issue, at that time. This divisive and unjust program continues today at the same pace with the same objectives. Left to the liberals it will continue regardless of cost and the injustices it promotes. Besides they have taken over control so effectively that no government could reverse the trend and restore equality of opportunity in a single term.

I also was aware of the duplicity of the bureaucracy in the implementation of B&B. You will remember when the Gens de l' Air and the Gens de la Mer raised the issue of using French in the Air in Quebec and on the St. Lawrence river by their river pilots and the government implemented it. There was a muted resistance in Transport Canada and the TSB even though we knew that safety would be compromised. Primarily in the air we prevent mid airs by the principle of see and be seen. Although this is backed up by traffic collision avoidance systems in some aircraft, radar in high traffic areas, and advisories from air traffic control it remains the final hope for avoiding collision. In this equation we rely, worldwide on the use of English so that all transmissions can be understood and pilots can keep track of other traffic. Obviously, if you do not understand other languages being used in the air then your ability to see and avoid is compromised. This situation persists today.

"The man who exercises discrimination pays a price for doing so."[9] Trudeau paid by almost being voted out in 1972 when he held on to power by two seats and by being rejected in 1979 but the price was far greater for Canada and we are still paying. It was the cost of keeping Quebec from separating, if you believe that possibility. Canada has paid dearly in a federal government filled with individuals unqualified for their jobs, taxpayer monies being squandered in Quebec through various job creation and sponsorship programs and countless contracts given to Quebec business without tender and without results. Every Canadian is paying for this man's arrogance and fortitude. We let him get away with it and we will have to set it straight. It will take us much longer to right the wrongs than it did for him to inflict them.

For a man who preached unity Trudeau was one of the most divisive prime ministers on record. "Unity" was his cloak but under it the magician hid his tools. His trademark was a rose in his lapel but beware the thorns! He fed the fires of division within this country. He bested the Provinces through the old method of divide and rule. He brought the West to its knees for the benefit of Central Canada. He coerced his government and the Canadian people through the use of rewards for loyalty and obedience. Unfortunately, the ineptitude of Joe Clark and his government's inability to count votes resulted in Trudeau's return. This gave him the opportunity to force the Constitutional issue and the entrenchment of equalization and the ability for governments to discriminate. Although he laments the notwithstanding clause, I remain sceptical. And Canadians need not bend to the prospect of Quebec leaving Canada because Quebecers would not sacrifice the standard of living they enjoy at others expense. It was always thus and it will remain so. However, the appeasement must end. Now the President of the Treasury Board, Madame Robillard is calling for all executives to be bilingual in the public service. The assault against English continues!

It is ironic however, that Ontarians, and Albertans, who finance Quebecers to the tune of approximately 5–6 billion in equalization payments every year are governed by the same Quebecers. Perhaps someday they will figure it out. In the meantime, the minority rules! And it is not pure generosity any more, Trudeau and the Provincial Premiers at the time, excepting Levesque, locked it into the constitution.

Trudeau set the tone and vision for the liberal party and that has not changed since his departure. In addition, most of his policies remain intact and certainly there has been no change in international policies. Granted, there have been pullbacks and reductions as a result of budget cuts and fiscal realities but the liberal party of today is essentially the same as he left it. Accordingly, I have made reference throughout to some of the more recent events and activities of the liberal party that find their genesis in the Trudeau era.

End Notes

1. Richard Gwyn, *"The Northern Magus,"* Toronto: McLelland and Stewart Ltd., 1980, p. 14.
2. Scott Reid, *"Lament For a Notion,"* Vancouver: Arsenal Pulp Press Ltd., 1993, p. 36.
3. Hayek, *"The Road to Serfdom,"* Chicago: The University of Chicago Press, 1994, p. 171.

4. William Gairdner, "*The Trouble with Canada,*" Toronto: General Paperbacks, 1991, pg. 11–12.
5. Pierre Trudeau, "*The Essential Trudeau,*" Toronto: McLelland and Stewart Ltd., 1998, p. 61.
6. Pierre Trudeau and Thomas Axworthy, "*Towards a Just Society,*" Toronto: McLelland and Stewart Ltd., 1993, p. 249.
7. Scott Reid, "*Lament for a Notion,*" Vancouver: Arsenal Pulp Press Ltd., 1993, p. 75.
8. Ibid., p. 77.
9. Milton Friedman, "*Capitalism and Freedom, 4th Ed.,*" Chicago: The University of Chicago Press, 2002, p. 110.

4

Centralization

In pursuing power Trudeau insisted and succeeded in increased centralization, thereby building large bureaucracies that subverted the provinces and municipalities and forced their dependence, through taxation, to the will of central Canada. In implementing equalization, and later including it in the repatriated constitution, he permanently seconded provincial power and placed a de facto provincial welfare system upon the state. In forty years of this forced system of robbing Peter to pay Paul or if you like, rewarding failure over success, he has created regional dependency where once regional pride reigned. At one time people moved where the employment was, they now choose to seek sustenance from social programs. Since Trudeau first took power we now have four generations of Canadians who have been inculcated with a social welfare mentality who believe it is a legitimate way to live. Fortunately, it does not appeal to everyone, yet.

In his book, *"The Road to Serfdom"*, F. A. Hayek describes the methodology of retreat into socialism and hence to Fascism or totalitarianism. Published in 1944 he has much to teach us about the problems of that period and how the Germans became victims of the lies of socialism.

In regards to character that is so important in the pursuit of progress he says:

> The virtues these people possessed-in a higher degree than most other people, excepting only a few of the smaller nations, like the Swiss and the Dutch-were independence and self-reliance, individual initiative and local responsibility, the successful reliance on voluntary activity, non-interference with one's neighbour and tolerance of the different and queer, respect for custom and tradition, and a healthy suspicion of power and authority. Almost all the traditions and institutions, in which democratic moral genius has found its most characteristic expression, are those which the progress of collectivism and its inherently centralistic tendencies are progressively destroying."[1]

Under Trudeau, some regions of Canada have lost this individuality and have become increasingly dependent on the largess of the central authority. At election time this takes the form of large spending campaigns to gain favour and votes. This activity has become a mainstay of Canadian and Liberal federal electoral practice. It favours overwhelmingly Quebec and the Atlantic Provinces.

The various methods to address regional disparities over successive liberal and conservative governments have taken the form of loans and grants or backing for various failed ventures. Atlantic Canada Opportunities Agency (ACOA), is the latest version of a long list of failed programs seeking to redress the Atlantic Provinces low economic output and high unemployment. Human Resources Development Commission (HRDC) has engaged in numerous make-work projects and job creation activities that would be more correctly termed waste management. That is the waste of taxpayer's money. Yet the socialists decry their virtue and shout down those who point out their inefficiencies and waste. Regrettably, the regions have become addicted to the handouts and have subverted their freedom and initiative to them. Anyone opposed is openly accused of racism, discrimination, or any other abuse or character flaw that seems appropriate. Unfortunately, these vulgar and false accusations are usually supported and amplified by the left leaning media in this country.

To make matters worse, equalization payments, no small amounts, were created to allow the various "have-not" provinces to provide similar federal services as the have provinces. For forty years now these monies have been transferred, from Alberta, Ontario, and occasionally British Columbia yet no change has occurred in the status of the have-nots in order that they can elevate themselves. Moreover, there is no auditing of these monies to determine if they are spent on federal services. They can be diverted wherever the provinces like. For example, in Quebec, they might fund the language police, education, or other activities that are not federally related. One must wonder how long the citizens of Alberta and Ontario will put up with this travesty in the name of social justice. They should take control of the system, since their citizens are funding it, and require an accounting and audit on an annual basis. Moreover, they should determine, in consultation with each have-not a schedule of removal from that status and termination of payments. One must understand that the standard of federal services in Alberta and Ontario are deprived as a result of these transfers. They find themselves in the curious situation, after the federal government of JC gutted the finances of Medicare in 1994, of waiting in infinite lines for medical services while others do not as a result of having their money transferred. It is all very curious why the citizens of Ontario and Alberta tolerate this injustice without a whimper. Is it their generosity or their stupidity?

Also, why should the federal government be in charge of the program? This is another example of the central government controlling through money allocation or taxing power another means of limiting Provincial power championed by Trudeau governments. Perhaps the worst example of central power abuse was the creation of the National Energy Program (NEP) wherein Ottawa dictated the price for oil in Canada regardless of the world price of oil. Based on false assumptions (oil would only increase in price and was not subject to the laws of supply and demand) this program was forced on the west to the benefit of central Canada (especially Quebec) in an attempt to reduce Provincial control over natural resources as guaranteed in the constitution. The feds were prepared to pay twice the amount per barrel to the Arabs than to our fellow Canadians. Meanwhile Albertans were forced to suffer the indignation and financial loss of billions in order to support central Canada, primarily Quebec. Along with that a federally owned oil company was created to thwart the external OPEC cartel but soon fell into step with the same, thus becoming a player in the rip off of the Canadian public. This was done to placate the NDP. "Between 1972 and 1974, when David Lewis and the New Democrats held the balance of power in Parliament, they put pressure on the government to create a crown corporation in the petroleum sector."[2] To this day the federal government resists all demands to reform this industry because of the tax revenues it gleans from the production, and distribution of oil. In the book "Towards a Just Society", Marc Lalonde, the Minister responsible at the time writes that the issue between Ottawa and Alberta was one of revenue sharing and "the Alberta government had to make room".[3]

The National Energy Program brought in new federal initiatives that were designed to "increase the federal share of revenue split".[4] This revenue grab was necessary because of the significant expenditures by the federal government on alternative sources of energy and the generous grants for substitutes. To offset this spending the revenues were needed to "reduce the federal deficit".[5] In addition, they were needed to redress the "increasing fiscal burden in the form of equalization programs."[6] In addition, the federal government allocated a 25% Crown share in frontier lands to themselves to ensure that future revenues would continue to flow.

This measure outraged the Alberta government as it effectively reduced Provincial jurisdiction over its constitutional guarantees over resources. A protracted and nasty struggle ensued between the two governments the results of which remain to this day in the form of western alienation. Fortunately, the assumptions underlying the program, as was so often the case with Trudeau's policies, were proved wrong and the oil shock was overcome by measures taken outside Canada and an oil glut ensued that resulted in much less revenue than was forecast. In retrospect Lalonde writes: "It was inevitable that there would be substantial criticism from Alberta when the federal government endeavoured to redistribute large amounts of wealth from that province where the oil and gas industry was heavily concentrated. I am sorry, however, that we could not persuade Albertans that the NEP had sufficient national merit to warrant their support and endorsement."[7] He went on to harshly criticize the Mulroney governments for their handling of the energy portfolio especially when free trade was achieved with the U.S. He predicted another energy crisis before the end of the decade and was convinced that Canada and the Western world were "pissing away" (his words) the increased oil sources found and developed by the NEP. Once again he has been proven wrong.

In retrospect the NEP did buy time in order to get the confused and contradictory liberal energy policy house in order but the public debate and the public squabble between Trudeau and Lougheed revealed the intransigence and conscious need that Trudeau saw himself and his Quebec lieutenants as the true guarantors for Quebec. In the initial stages of this crisis Quebec benefited from the cheaper Middle Eastern oil but when the prices exceeded those set by the federal government domestically, the oil pipeline from Sarnia to Montreal was quickly completed so that Quebec could choose the cheapest supply source for the remainder of the crisis. In the end it was a very costly program which increased the taxes on Canadians and the debt of the federal government. The harm it did to intergovernmental relations lives on. Michael Bliss sums up the NEP as follows: "Everything else about the NEP crashed into ruins and disrepute in 1981, as it turned out that the intellectual foundation of the government's energy strategy was completely fallacious. ... The whole energy-planning elite had failed to understand elementary market economics."[8]

Given the centralization that has taken place since Trudeau entered the picture it is easy to see where central planning has moved into every area of Canadian life and thereby has reduced initiative and self-reliance of the public. Not content to rule with an iron fist over its constitutional jurisdictions the feds have taken over our lives and impinged on our individual freedoms. Collective rights have taken priority over individual rights to the detriment of all. Interest groups sprung up like weeds in the Trudeau public policy garden and most were fertilized by the federal government creating many more new jobs for the in crowd and more spending for the public treasury. The status of women is a good example wherein increased emphasis was placed up and to the point of creating a Minister as well as divisions within each government department. But why should the government fund special interest groups? They don't speak for the average citizen and if their cause is just why can't they raise funds from their supporters? There is no reason why the taxpayer should be asked to fund these single issue groups that are generally seeking to pursue their own narrow self interest. Yet Trudeau and subsequent governments financed their conferences, trips abroad and other activities that often criticized Canada and her policies.

A more recent example in the same vein is Bill C 68 in that the federal government, aided by a liberal judiciary appointed by the government, have forced gun registration upon its citizens, at a cost far exceeding promised, (85 million stated and now approaching one billion and still counting) with biased and false statistics, and portraying those most responsible with firearms as the problem. The program has not, nor will not, prevent crimes because the criminals won't participate. It is the height of folly perpetrated on a dumb and gullible public probably with the main hidden goal of disarming citizens. We shall see! So far it has cost close to a billion dollars and less than one third of gun owners have come forward. Even in this the government continues to produce false claims. The point is that this is just another example of the Trudeau style applied today.

Central Planning is the bedrock on which socialism is structured. Why would anyone think that something as complex as an economy and a political system that is supposed to serve a diverse country with many regional differences and communities could be run better by a bloated bureaucracy centered on a federal system? If the municipalities and provinces are to have meaning then the more planning that can be accomplished there should be the preference. However, socialists have a different view and we can all see the benefits such as the quality of life in Russia, the previous Soviet Union, China, and Cuba etc. Most everyone is familiar with the Great Leap Forward in China and the failed five year plans of the

Soviet Union. These disasters were the brilliant product of central planning under socialist and communist regimes. But the true virtue of central planning from a socialist view is the power that it generates. Once again if we examine the NEP of Trudeau we can see the benefits accrued to Central Canada at the expense of the West. Quebec could buy oil from the Middle East or from Alberta, whichever was cheaper and although at the start of the oil crisis the oil pipeline did not extend to Montreal it was soon built to permit this preferential pricing to La Belle Province. If you wonder why this was done just consider where the power and support for the liberal party came in those elections. It came from Quebec where the majority of cabinet members also emerged under Trudeau.

Central planning in Trudeau's government brought us to our knees with national debt under the stewardship of JC as our finance minister and after years of fumbling and bumbling with the economy the feds were forced to invoke wage and price controls which confirmed that their economic plans had failed. This was chaotic for the economy as we went from full steam ahead to full reverse. Concurrently Mr. Crow, the head of our central bank myopically pursued inflation with a vengeance which brought the economy to its knees. The runaway inflation brought on by the unrestrained federal spending once again required the strongest possible monetary policy in order to bring it within acceptable levels. At the time the government, as one would expect, cast blame to anyone and anything that the unwashed would accept instead of facing up to their own incompetence. There is some truth that the oil crisis was to blame but the NEP resulted in a large spending program by the government on alternative sources, our very own Oil Company and grants for substitutes. All of this fuelled the fire of inflation.

Similarly collective bargaining in the public service

was suspended for several years in the 90's which also demonstrated the failure of this Trudeau program. How could it have been successful when only the government had bargaining power? Oh sure, the workers had the right to strike but when they exercised it they were usually legislated back to work which put the lie to that part of the program. The Treasury Board is still trying to develop a workable model for the Public Service that will restore morale and credibility after the failed programs and social engineering anchored in the Trudeau era. Billions in planning costs and consulting fees were committed in the last decade on the new "Universal Classification System" only to have it flounder when it was rejected as unacceptable by management. The public and public service anxiously await the next management marvel to emerge from the planning desks where policy is based on confrontation rather than co-operation.

Professor Milton Friedman in his book *"Capitalism and Freedom"* captures the essence of government and what happens to unfettered power when he states:

> Government is necessary to preserve our freedom, it is an instrument through which we can exercise our freedom; yet by concentrating power in political hands, it is also a threat to freedom. Even though the men who wield this power initially be of good will and even though they be not corrupted by the power they exercise, the power will both attract and form men of a different stamp.[9]

This is a critical comment that goes to the heart of how we need to exercise judgment on who we select to wield this power. It also points out the need to impose limits on the time that individuals can spend in the political arena. In Canada it has become customary to see some people spend their entire careers in politics some without ever having done a real job. Moreover, until recently the senate was peopled by young individuals who were there for life. A more recent rule forces their retirement at age 75. Nonetheless, these people are already party loyalists who will not change nor are they likely to bring anything new to the political arena. In short, they are in retirement and if they do nothing, and many do, there are no consequences. This is a tremendous waste of potential in government but as long as the party system keeps a stranglehold on politics then nothing will change.

The omnipresent control of government holds this country back in many ways. At the UN we pride ourselves in setting on the fence. The number of abstains in our voting record testifies to our inability to decide and/or our hesitancy to offend. We want to be seen as the honest broker but our actions reveal that we are reluctant to take a stand. Economically we are backward. We watch others to see if they succeed with their new approaches before we decide to change. I witnessed this while working with the TSB. I noted that Transport Canada would not react to safety concerns unless the Americans, the UK, or the Aussies did so first and preferably all three. Management in that organization was unwilling to take most risks. This approach was ironic in an industry that makes decisions every day based on risk analysis. In banking the government stops the banks from merging even though their analysis shows that to compete globally they must do so. In EI, Medicare, and Provincial Vehicle Insurance programs the government forces private industry out at the expense of the public. The government by creating monopolies wastes resources. Besides that many of the social programs such as Canada Pension Plan, Employment Insurance, etc., are not voluntary. Thus, the government takes your money, puts it into general revenue and hopes to have the resources in the future to pay you back. On the other hand, insurance companies and you are likely to invest those premiums which support the economy to a far greater extent than government expenditures. Again, this represents a net loss to Canada's macro economy. The fact that you might be able to do better is disregarded for the "greater good". In short, your freedom to choose how you want to provide for your medical treatment, car insurance, unemployment, retirement, and other aspects of your life are restricted. These examples are clearly coercion by government on your freedom. Moreover, they represent a reduction on your income that further restricts your freedom since you might have used it to purchase things more relevant to you.

The other element in the quote is the tendency to attract the wrong kind of people to government; those who wish to control, those who covet power, those who will subvert the state to their desires, those who will lavish gifts on their friends or supporters, those who will use their power to corrupt others, those who will lie to preserve their station, those who will eventually see themselves above the law, and those who will commit crimes against the State. Recently, we had five convicted felons serving in the Senate. A jury of peers had found them guilty yet they remain in the Senate drawing their salary. Meanwhile the current liberal government is beset by scandals and police investigations into their activities and the current Prime Minister is one who has had some shady dealing in his interest in a golf course. His explanations and the paper work stretch the bounds of credulity. This government's actions and lack of accountability seem to confirm the merit of Professor Friedman's statement, at least in Canada.

End Notes

1. Hayek, "*The Road to Serfdom*," Chicago: University of Chicago Press, 1994, p. 235.
2. James Laxer, "*In Search of a New Left*," Toronto: Penguin Books, 1997, p.174.
3. Pierre Trudeau and Thomas Axworthy, "*Towards a Just Society*," Toronto: McLelland and Stewart Ltd., 1993, p. 108.
4. Ibid., p. 109.
5. Ibid., p. 109.
6. Ibid., p. 109.
7. Ibid., p. 118.
8. Michael Bliss, "*Right Honourable Men*," Toronto: HarperCollins, 1995, p. 270.
9. Milton Friedman, "*Capitalism and Freedom, 4th Ed.*," Chicago: University of Chicago Press, 2002, p. 2.

5

Socialism and Freedom are Mutually Exclusive

De Tocqueville was clear in his appraisal that democracy and socialism were poles apart. He said in 1848 that "Democracy extends the sphere of individual freedom, socialism restricts it. Democracy attaches all possible value to each man; socialism makes each man a mere agent, a mere number. Democracy and socialism have nothing in common but one word: equality. But notice the difference: while democracy seeks equality in liberty, socialism seeks equality in restraint and servitude." Professor Hayek in quoting De Tocqueville lays bare the dilemma or choice that citizens must make eventually in their pursuit of equality. At the heart of democracy and our constitution is the concept of private property that allows people to succeed or fail as the fates allow. But socialism strips that away over time. "In this sense socialism means the abolition of private enterprise, of private ownership of the means of production, and the creation of a system of "planned economy" in which the entrepreneur working for profit is replaced by a central planning body."[1]

Socialism is addictive. It may start out as a small intrusion into the freedom of the people or the freedom of the marketplace but once in the system it takes possession of the body and then the mind. It replaces competition in the market and freedom of choice. Socialism is usually presented as the desire for equality. But it can never provide equality but only a system that is considered more equal. This is an approach that sets people apart rather than one that seeks to bring them together. It sets man against man, region against region, and country against country. It usually comes to us from politicians who promise "social justice" or the "common good", those catchy phrases that Trudeau always used and campaigned successfully on.

Socialism is a system whereby the privileged few decide for the unprivileged many. The great equalizer is taxes whereby the haves support the have-nots. And the have-nots become eventually the will-nots since they are guaranteed at least a minimal standard of living for doing absolutely nothing. The incipient spiral into socialism results from its attractiveness for the indigent, the ne'er-do-wells, the malcontents, the opportunists and the clever but lazy in our midst. As we have seen in Canada it becomes easier to demand that the government solve our problems than to resort to our own initiative. In order to do that the government must plan more and therefore needs more planners. Similarly, the government needs more ministers and departments as new issues emerge but rarely abolishes departments as issue fade. All of this takes money and results in higher borrowing or higher taxes or both. But the reality is this, "once government has embarked upon planning for the sake of justice, it cannot refuse responsibility for anybody's fate or position."[2] Hence, you witness the government coming to the aid of businesses big and small and individuals because it is the government that has partly created the failures and have accepted responsibility for all. We rise and fall on the governments plans.

One final point regarding the government's intrusion

into our lives that restricts our freedom is the myth of private property. Property taxes are nothing more than rent. If you fail to pay them then the government will confiscate your land. If you wish to remain a property "owner" then you must meet the government's demands and they are ever increasing. If you rent or lease you still pay taxes indirectly to the landlord so you see the concept of private property is passé. You cannot now even alter your property without permission of several government agencies. Finally, it is becoming more and more difficult to pass on your property to your relatives through the ever changing rules or taxes related to estates.

When we were free, it was possible to make our own decisions and carry them through, to succeed or fail on our own and no one much bothered. Today, creeping socialism brings us more and more into each others lives. We are becoming experts at minding other peoples business. Special interests, often funded by government, have sprung up everywhere and sometimes seek to alter society even through violence. The government is forced to move into areas where other institutions were once unchallenged. Moral issues are now fair game for society at large where once they were influenced primarily by religion. Justice is dispensed today by a system filled with political appointees rather than by those who have risen in rank due to merit. Once appointed, they are expected to follow the line of government, again the few deciding for the many.

A case in point of how incipient and how quickly socialism can take control can be found in Newfoundland & Labrador. Our junior province, they joined confederation in 1949 under the liberal banner. At the time they were self-sufficient and self-reliant. Over time they sold their rights in Labrador to the Churchill Falls. It was a bad deal for them but a good one for Quebec. Despite several attempts to right this wrong the Quebec government, with the aid of the federal government, have consistently refused to reopen this agreement. Then, Newfoundland relied on the fishing and lumber industry. But the federal government began to take over more and more the planning and control of the fishery. Today it is extinct. Likewise, the lumber industry is in trouble due to the intrusion of government. Today the Newfoundland government is involved with offshore oil but since most of the Capital was put up by the oil companies and the federal government, it is them that will reap the reward. In another act of faith the current government is negotiating another Churchill River power project with Quebec. In another they are about to sign a deal with a mining firm that promises to build a smelter in Labrador at some future date in order to provide jobs. I hope this time they do better on these projects than before but with the federal liberals also involved I doubt that Newfoundland and Labrador will get a fair shake. I would bet on Quebec and the mining company to prevail. If I am wrong I will be as happy as the Newfoundlanders.

   In other parts of the country we see failure of central planning as well. The wheat board has lost the trust of the farmers but the farmers have no choice, they must market their product through the Wheat Board. Similarly, marketing boards for eggs, poultry, pork, etc., restrict product in order to keep prices high. The taxpayer is denied imports and gets higher prices for domestic product. The lack of government support for farmers and successive years of drought has landed that industry in crisis. Medicare became a monopoly under the Pearson government. Despite the abundant evidence that monopolies are destructive because they squeeze out competition and result in unsustainable costs, this program has come to crisis as well. This is as a result of costs which should be no surprise. As Trudeau points out in his "Memoirs" "Mr. Pearson had the House pass the health insurance bill, but he refrained from having it proclaimed law because no one had any idea what its financial consequences would be." Trudeau went on to pass the law but without financial costing in the short or long term. Although he goes on to state that after that he made sure that proper costing was made for future programs it is clear that that is not the case because with each new program we see constant increases in either taxes (education) or premiums (CPP, EI, etc.) to fund the progressively increasing costs for these programs. And just a note on EI as it is now tagged; it is interesting to note that no one has a choice on participation. If you work you pay into it. It also takes the form of robbing Peter to pay Paul with high wage earners not subject to layoffs supporting the obverse. If it were voluntary many citizens would not participate. Moreover, neither would many of the business who must pay as well. In short, it is not an insurance program it is a tax.

To make matters worse a socialist has been appointed as a one man band to solve the problem Medicare program. As a socialist he is not likely to bring any new proposals to a program that needs a heavy infusion of reality. In the absence of government capacity the people have introduced two and three tier health care while the federal government pointed their accusatory finger at the Provinces. Why is it wrong to have a choice for those who are sick between private and public health care? Is it not possible to blend the two which will take place anyway despite the poor planning of governments? And who should decide the people or the privileged few? Is it ethical for this power to reside with politicians alone because through socialism they have removed our freedom to choose what kind of health care we want to have? You as a citizen, with limited freedom, have the right to choose who you want to govern you. Beware of those who promise "social justice" a "balanced approach" or programs for the "common good". They are charlatans seeking your power that they may use for their own purposes. Make them state their plans and how they intend to pay for them and that they will give you a final input before implementation. Not a mere vote by their party members but a referendum. Surely your health care and how it is going to be funded and run is worthy of your vote.

It is ironic that in a country where we have enjoyed freedom that has been the result of democracy and capitalism we should think that socialism will deliver anything better. Moreover, we hardly question those who propose it even though there are unlimited examples of its failure to provide anything of the kind. "Because we live in a largely free society, we tend to forget how limited is the span of time and the part of the globe for which there has ever been anything like political freedom: the typical state of mankind is tyranny, servitude, and misery."[3] Just look at Africa today or many parts of Asia and you will realize that there are two distinct ways of governing with two distinct results. "Fundamentally there are only two ways of coordinating the economic activities of millions. One is central direction involving the use of coercion — the technique of the army and of the modern totalitarian state. The other is voluntary co-operation of individuals — the technique of the market place."[4] I doubt that many Canadians would choose to relocate to these locations; indeed millions are trying to relocate to Canada and Western states where democracy and restrained capitalism are the chosen ways to govern. Liberals should reflect on this demographic fact!

End Notes

1. Hayek, "*The Road to Serfdom,*" Chicago: University of Chicago Press, 1994, p. 37.
2. Ibid., p. 118.
3. Milton Friedman, "*Capitalism and Freedom, 4th Ed.,*" Chicago: University of Chicago Press, 2002, p. 9.
4. Ibid., p. 13.

6

Principles and Ethics

The current government and the PM (a PET disciple) pride themselves on their pragmatism. The unfortunate aspect is that one that is pragmatic is often without principle:

> The principle that the end justifies the means in individualist ethics is regarded as the denial of all morals. In collectivist ethics it becomes necessarily the supreme rule; there is literally nothing which the consistent collectivist must not be prepared to do if it serves "the good of the whole," because the "good of the whole" is to him the only criterion of what ought to be done. The reason d'etat, in which collectivist ethics has found its most explicit formulation, knows no other limit than that set by expediency–... There can be no limit to what its citizen must be prepared to do, no act which his conscience must prevent him from committing, if it is necessary for an end which the community has set itself or which his superiors order him to achieve." "Political freedom means the absence of coercion of a man by his fellow men. The fundamental threat to freedom is power to coerce, be it in the hands of a monarch, a dictator, an oligarchy, or a momentary majority.[1]

The worst example of this expediency and lack of principle was the implementation of B&B back in the early 70's. Merit was struck down, although repeatedly denied by the government and the bureaucracy mandarins, as the guiding principle in the achievement of promotion or hiring in the federal public service. In addition, 28% of all jobs in all classifications were to go to, a French mother tongue determination, at the time this constituted 28% of the population. That has now dropped to below 25% nevertheless the target has not been lowered, and at all levels within the public service. The net result is a demoralized federal public service, RCMP, and Canadian Forces who have seen the meteoric rise of individuals within their ranks whose prime qualification is their mother tongue. Since then the government has followed up with affirmative action programs for women, visible minorities, and native Canadians. The docile public was appeased by the bilingual provisions of the policy which have been a monumental failure at great expense to the taxpayers of Canada. Successful propaganda by the government led the people to believe that this program was in their best interest or "the common good" and anyone who was against it was labelled racist. The real goal, biculturalism, remained cloaked in fog.

Pragmatism at worst negates principles and values and at best compromises them. Again William Gairdner has captured the national approach to pragmatism and the problems that emerge there from:

> We do not fancy ourselves to be an ideologically sophisticated or politically strident people. Rather, we like to think we are "pragmatic." But I fear that pragmatism — the search for practical solutions — may also be a self-congratulatory label camouflaging a national intellectual laziness. I would go even further and say that our pride in pragmatic solutions to political and social problems makes it especially difficult for us to see beneath the surface, and thus we are vulnerable to

the gradualism relied upon by social engineers. They know that we can be easily distracted by the din and uproar of the game — while they quietly change the rules. With pragmatism as a national philosophy, you can certainly win a lot of short-term battles, but without a solid set of commonly upheld national values, standards, and institutions, you risk losing the war.[2]

Trudeau was very aware of the vulnerability of Canadian society and their erroneous belief that the English had wronged the French. In addition he introduced, after the B&B commission wrongly concluded, that this nation was founded by two nations. If this falsehood could be hammered into the English heads then the demands of the French would be easier to deliver. In addition, with the low quality of individuals elected as MPs, not well educated in political philosophy or political economy, and easily manipulated into believing that the French deserved more from confederation than others, Trudeau was able to execute his conspiracy with the help of the English. For example, "while the NDP had adopted the view that Canada constituted "two nations" in its found program of 1961, ... "[3]

Again, Richard Gwyn captures the importance of B&B to Trudeau. "Bilingualism is to Trudeau as the CPR to John A. Macdonald, his instrument for building a continent-wide country out of a huddled group of provinces."[4] This was Trudeau's end and the means was B&B. That the means was immoral and ruined hundreds of thousands of careers of Anglophones while vaulting hundreds of thousands of Francophones careers was irrelevant to Trudeau and his minions. His purpose was to establish the French fact and nothing would dissuade him. He rarely justified B&B and if he commented it was to downplay its importance and all the while his minions were employing every possible ploy or method to hasten its implementation. It turned into a feeding frenzy that has cost the taxpayers billions.

Trudeau makes no apologies for his appointments of French Canadians ahead of others more qualified. In *"The Essential Trudeau"*, he states: "When I became prime minister, I was always trying to move French-speaking Canadians into posts they had never occupied in Ottawa. At one point we had a French-speaking governor general, prime minister, chief of defence staff, head of the RCMP, minister of finance, and so on."[5] While he went to great pains to dispute that Quebecers had no special status nor should they expect one he aggressively sought opportunities to ensure they were favoured. "Our government also worked to foster the growth of an entrepreneurial class in Quebec. The first initiative was made through its Crown corporations. We made efforts to establish a base for the transportation industry in Montreal. We named French Canadians to head Air Canada, the CNR, and the communications networks. Second, we alerted our ministers and bureaucrats to the presence of excellent entrepreneurs in Quebec, in order to steer some federal contracts their way."[6] By his acts rather than his words Trudeau rapidly secured special status for Quebec and Quebecers while favouring Quebec industry while starting the politicization of the bureaucracy. More recently through the auspices of Public Works we see that funnelling monies into Quebec continues unabated and yet no one accounts for it or accepts responsibility for it. The people who are responsible and accountable are unwilling to tell us how this took place even though they supposedly work for us. I hope the *honourable* past minister of Public Works is enjoying his exile in Denmark.

That Trudeau politicized the bureaucracy is not in dispute. When Joe Clark came to power he fired Michael Pitfield, who was the first Chief of the Privy Council to be terminated due to partisanship. In *"The Northern*

Magus", Richard Gwyn writes: "During the Pitfield-Robertson era, the top ranks of the civil service became indistinguishable, for all practical purposes, from the Liberal Party. Trudeau's political aides moved into top civil service positions, and vice versa; a deputy minister, Jack Austin, became Trudeau's chief of staff. Liberals were allowed to parachute themselves into almost any public service post they wanted — ex-minister Bryce McCaskey's appointment as Chairman of Air Canada being the most blatant example — and did so to a degree unequalled since the establishment of the civil service merit principle in 1918."[7] Gwyn goes on to demonstrate that by reorganizing the cabinet committees and bringing in senior civil servants as ministerial experts for support, Trudeau unwittingly allowed bureaucrats to "enter the mainstream of political decision-making and were all the influential... they were so adroitly deferential." [8] We see today the continuation of these policies in the placing of liberals in executive positions within the civil service and in contracting by the Department of Public Works, and other departments as well. The continuation of these policies was seen in the Conservative government of Brian Mulroney as well whereby with the letting of F-18 fighter maintenance to Bombardier rather than the better tender of Bristol of Winnipeg the alienation of western Canada was again aggravated. For anyone who doubts this favouritism and appalling lack of oversight and management by government they need only read the annual Auditor General's (AG) reports.

    In the campaign against separation enormous sums were spent by the federal government to ensure that Quebecers would know that they could expect money and more from the federal government if they voted to remain in Canada. Even after Trudeau stated that Separatism "died in 1976 and was buried by the referendum in 1980" we find ourselves today spending vast sums of money in Quebec under the Canada Sponsorship program. And yes, most of it falls outside the rules and guidelines published by Treasury Board and influenced by Francophone public servants who according to the AG "broke every rule in the book".

In addition, and as a sop to those of other ethnic origins, multiculturalism was introduced and supported to a far lesser degree, thus creating the illusion that everyone could have a piece of this program. In describing multiculturalism it took on a decidedly anti-American flavour: "With its adoption, we, unlike our American neighbours, were declining to sacrifice our multicultural wealth and diversity in the name of national unity. We were renouncing the notion of a cultural monolith, of an American-style melting-pot. We were espousing the principle that a free and just society must accept pluralism and allow each citizen to make a personal choice of suitable lifestyle, customs, and culture, whether or not these flowed from his or her own ethnicity."[9] This policy received unanimous support in Parliament even though it sacrificed national unity. If you are trying to unite the country, as Trudeau often challenged, why would you pass legislation that effectively disunites it. Clearly, there was and remains much ambiguity in this policy and especially when you consider that taxpayers are funding every culture claimed. Granted there should be no force applied to compel immigrants to adopt Canadian culture, whatever that is, yet on the other hand, nor should there be incentives for them to perpetuate the culture they abandoned, left, or escaped.

Unfortunately, monies spent on multiculturalism were also a deception but enough to appease the media, the elite, and those who didn't know any better. In taxpayer's dollars, those spent on multiculturalism were and are a drop in the barrel compared to those squandered on B&B. In, *"Lament for a Notion"*, Scott Reid applied a reasonable model in an attempt to quantify the cost of bilingualism from 1974 to 1992, despite the lack of accurate accounting from the federal government he found:

> On this basis, the total cumulative cost of federal languages policy from the beginning of the Trudeau years to today has been the addition of 49 billion to the federal debt, billons more to various provincial debts, and a permanent loss to Canadian consumers of $40 billion worth of consumption.[10]

Using these figures we can extrapolate that it has cost about $2.7 billion a year for bilingualism so that by today in 2002 we have spent another $27 billion for a total of $76 billion and a loss to Canadian consumers of an additional $20 billion worth of consumption for a total of $60 billion. This is a tremendous loss especially when we consider that it came from borrowed money thereby raising interest rates and requiring interest to be paid. To put these amounts in perspective consider that the federal government expenditure is approximately $120 billion per annum today. Therefore, we have spent approximately two years worth of federal government expenditures on this program or three if we use 1985 expenditures. Moreover, since we went in debt to finance it, some of the approximately $40 billion we pay annually in interest on our accumulated debt goes to service monies used to finance this program. And what have we got to show for it besides Quebecers running the country and the call for even more in the public service? There is no way that this can be justified and to continue at the present rate is irresponsible and reprehensible. It demonstrates how totally duped the Canadian public has been over the years over this program. Another way of looking at this colossal waste is the "alternative costs" theory in economics. Just think of the material benefit to Canada if these monies were either not borrowed or were invested in projects that gave some return on investment.

As an investment in human capital they have benefited only a small segment of our society and the return has been insignificant. In short, a loss unequalled except perhaps by two world wars where the cost in lives is incalculable.

Bear in mind that this does not represent the cost of biculturalism. Nor the cost of needless translation of documents that gather dust. If you are curious about these costs, Reid includes an appendix in his book that details, again as best can be extrapolated from the fog of data, the cost of some specific translation projects and an overall estimate from Treasury Board for translation costs in one year alone. These continuing costs are unnecessary for the most part and constitute another make work project for bilingual Canadians. If parliamentarians were asked to spend these funds, given the utility received, they would reject it outright if it was their money. Since it is ours and a rejection would cause objections, they remain silent. A reasonable person would conclude that the extreme difficulty in cost accounting bilingualism since its inception is that the government doesn't want you to know the real cost. Hence, the deception in the accounting.

Bilingualism was an end *unjustified* by the means but partly justifiable nonetheless if it had been thought out and implemented properly at the time. In retrospect if the monies squandered on the francophone teachers, the infrastructure, translators, and the public service, which continues today but to a lesser extent than in the heady 70's, had been directed to the Canadian educational system and the curriculum and teachers were prepared properly for the task we would have by now achieved the target for those under 30 years of age. Instead, we have a multitude of retired and serving members of the public service who for the most part never achieved real bilingualism aghast at the wasted effort. Nonetheless, the liberals soldier on trying to achieve the unachievable by employing their usual tactic of throwing money at the problem. As a job creation program for Quebecers it was most successful and still is. I am aware that education is a provincial responsibility but a standard education across Canada is a worthwhile national objective and if you dangle that kind of money in front of the Provinces, they would accept; except of course, Quebec who would opt out, without financial penalty.

Of course, the current example of the lack of ethics of our current socialist government is the scandal ridden cabinet and HRDC frauds. Much of this can be traced to those beneficiaries of B&B who are now so prominent within the government and the bureaucracy. As further evidence of the degree to which the bureaucracy has been politicized, take the current example of the two francophone executives who were executive-directors in charge of the sponsorship program post-referendum and were found to have "broken all the rules" of financial and program planning. But when testifying before the House of Commons committee on 9 Jul 02 they were unable to remember any details. One of them refused to answer questions on the advice of his lawyer which despite the legality involved is an insult to Canadians and Parliament. This and other scandals such as the letting of taxpayer monies by the corrections department without tender clearly demonstrate that the bureaucracy is out of control and the Treasury Board who is supposedly in charge is unable to exercise command and control over the situation. Either that or the liberals have managed to establish the kind of waste management they prefer. In any event, taxpayer money from the most overtaxed people in the G8 continues to be flushed down the sewer from Ottawa to Quebec and beyond.

We will have to wait some time for the documentation to be released from the Secrecy of the Cabinet before we will get a true picture of one of the worst examples of excess that took place in Quebec in 1970. A provincial government in trouble with a reputed corrupt police force when faced with a small cell of terrorists, the FLQ, overreacted and called on the federal government to intercede. Pierre Elliot Trudeau (PET), for reasons still known only to him, invaded Quebec, instituted martial law, rounded up many opponents to the government along with many private citizens, still not aware of why they were detained, and held them against their will until the crisis was over. The incident and the documentation, if it still exists, have not been released. But one thing is sure, that it is a classical example of using a howitzer to stamp out a fly. We shall see, but it had every appearance of PET rising to a dare by a newsman and a means to show Quebecers that the federal government was the only one that could really protect them. It may well have elements also, of upstaging a political opponent, in the then impotent and vacillating Premier Robert Bourassa. One thing is telling and that is that one cannot find any significant reference to it in Trudeau's writings or those of his unabashed worshipers.

That Trudeau was left alone to decide what to do in the absence of good intelligence, an inept federal police force, a reportedly corrupt provincial one, and a provincial government unable to come to terms with their crisis, which had been ongoing for some years, is made clear in his memoirs. In the absence of a less draconian law, which the War Measures Act was, it is clear that by the time he took charge the situation was critical. He did what he did to show the world, particularly the U.S., that Canada was not in crisis and that these terrorists would be brought to justice. He did succeed but at great cost to Canada and her sense of security. In time we will know the full story, perhaps. We do know that the perpetrators were hardly brought to justice.

The FLQ crisis, as it was known demonstrates another facet of socialist regimes and that is their propensity to distort the truth in order to achieve their goals. Again,

Professor Hayek states: "It is essential that the people should come to regard them as their own ends. Although the beliefs must be chosen for the people and imposed upon them, they must become their beliefs, a generally accepted creed which makes the individuals as far as possible act spontaneously in the way the planner wants."[11] The FLQ crisis was cloaked in secrecy, and still is, with only those elements exposed that supported the government's actions. The people, to almost total exclusion, were kept from the truth that a small group of amateur terrorists could paralyze a country and bring on the War Measures Act to stamp out this "apprehended insurrection."

There are many citizens who had their basic freedoms trampled on by this abuse of power and are still seeking the facts that required its use. In the aftermath other governments have brought in the Emergencies Act in order to deal with similar situations without resorting to what was in effect Marshall Law. The suspicions still remain though that this draconian act by PET was an exercise of his ego to demonstrate his willingness to exercise power in the absence of action by Quebec's Premier and at the same time cover-up the ineptitude of police forces who should have eradicated the FLQ long before.

Trudeau and his government lacked the understanding, or just ignored it, that their role was not to interfere in the democratic process by discriminating against some for the benefit of others or to try to control and manipulate in areas where freedom should prevail. Their task and the task of any democratic government is more limited but also more important. "In summary, the organization of economic activity through voluntary exchange presumes that we have provided, through government, for the maintenance of law and order to prevent coercion of one individual by another, the enforcement of contracts voluntarily entered into, the definition of the meaning of property rights, the interpretation and enforcement of such rights, and the provision of a monetary framework."[12] As demonstrated Trudeau's government was the instrument of coercion, it was the instrument of inflation through unreasonable deficits and debt accumulation, and it was the enforcer of its own discrimination. Moreover, failure to provide better law and order by their inability to effectively thwart terror earlier by the FLQ, through the federal police force, parts of Quebec and Ontario were subjected to Marshall Law whereby citizens lost their civil rights for a time. This was not "peace, order and good government," nor was it democracy.

End Notes

1. Milton Friedman, "*Capitalism and Freedom, 4th Ed.*," Chicago: University of Chicago Press, 2002, p. 15.
2. William Gairdner, "*The Trouble with Canada*," Toronto: General Paperbacks, 1991, p. 97.
3. James Laxer, "*In Search of the New Left*," Toronto: Penguin Books, 1997, p.157.
4. Richard Gwyn, "*The Northern Magus*," Toronto: McLelland and Stewart, 1980, p. 220.
5. Pierre Trudeau, "*The Essential Trudeau*," Toronto: McLelland and Stewart, 1998, p. 160.
6. Ibid., p. 107.
7. Richard Gwyn, "*The Northern Magus*," Toronto: McLelland and Stewart, 1980, p. 78.
8. Ibid., p. 88.
9. Pierre Trudeau and Thomas Axworthy, "*Towards a Just Society*", Toronto: Penguin Books, 1992, p. 182.
10. Scott Ried, "*Lament for a Notion*," Vancouver: Arsenal Pulp Press, 1993, p. 250.
11. Hayek, "*The Road to Serfdom*," Chicago: University of Chicago Press, 1994, p. 168.
12. Milton Friedman, "*Capitalism and Freedom, 4th Ed.*," Chicago: University of Chicago Press, 2002, p. 27.

7

Truth and Trudeau

Have you ever wondered why politicians lie so much? Is it because they are so altruistic that they wish to protect the population from the ugly truth? Well they may want you to believe so but that is not the reason. To politicians truth is silly putty. They can shape it into any form they wish and do so all the time; this is known as spin. For myself as soon as I hear a denial from a politician I assume that there is at least an 80% chance that the denial confirms the rumour or fact. On the other hand, if a confirmation is made then conversely there is an 80% chance that it is a lie. Why is this so?

Simply put it is because the politicians will go to extremes to shield the public from finding out how incompetent and inept they really are. Unfortunately, they have learned to use the media, some of whom they control, to aid them in their unending deceptions. Only a handful of really good investigative reporters and producers can get to the truth but by the time it is presented the public has usually moved on. However, there is another reason. The truth is very hard to find and even harder to deal with. As a consequence, we prefer lies and secrecy.

Cabinet secrecy prevents the public or the media from learning the truth about government decisions. If that cannot be invoked then there is always the resort to closure in Parliament to ensure that a subject or bill receives minimal debate; a tactic that grew exponentially under Trudeau's leadership. More recently we have a new measure, the termination of a public inquiry. The Somalia inquiry was terminated early not because of the time or expense, as suggested by the liberals but because it was getting too close to the truth and the architects of the strategy. Goodness knows other inquiries have taken much longer and cost considerably more but none were on the precipice of exposing the perpetrators as was the case here. By shutting it down the government sent the wrong message to the military and the bureaucracy; stonewall and ye shall be taken care of. You will remember that for all the wrongdoing only one private went to jail. Many military officers had their careers ruined but no civilians were punished, in fact, many were promoted, such as the DM who was well connected to the powerful through marriage. All in all, the Somalia inquiry was a travesty to public accountability. Only the military lost, as well as truth. For a detailed account of the Somalia inquiry debacle, I recommend *"Somalia Cover-Up: A Commissioner's Journal"* by Peter Desbarats.

In a similar case, also involving the military, when the ill-conceived and totally inept UN peacekeeping mission in Rwanda failed completely Canadian military officers who were directly involved, in particular the mission commander and the senior Canadian military advisor in New York, were promoted by the Canadian government. These individuals who at best could be excused due to lack of experience were elevated within the military to the highest ranks in an effort to overshadow their involvement. Today one still struggles with the psychological aftermath of his experience. The other continues to enjoy the confidence of the government and serves as a highly paid consultant. At the same time civilians at the UN who were similarly implicated also received promotions. These actions confirm the government's inability to account for its failures and accept responsibility accordingly. Instead they spin. UN missions have been notorious for lack of planning and execution since they began and despite the lessons learned the Canadian government continues to support the UN and expose Canadian personnel to undue risk. The truth is the lessons have not been learned and corrective actions have rarely been taken by either the Canadian Forces or the UN.

Finally, we have the long list of political promises forgotten or ignored when power was achieved through the election. Too many to mention however, a few stand out such as Wage & Price controls. I will leave you to ferret out the others. It helps confirm why the electorate continues to avoid the voting polls since they cannot believe much of anything said during a campaign. In that vein Trudeau aggravated an already bad situation. The public has always been wary of politicians and their promises but Trudeau plumbed new lows in lack of credibility. By the time he retired the pubic had gone through stages of disillusion, disgust, and finally contempt. This was due in large measure to what Barlow and Campbell described as "policy schizophrenia"[1] They went on to state their case:

> Trudeau's policies and public musings were all over the map. He would defend social programs and cut social programs; he would raise corporate taxes and cut corporate taxes; he would lecture the business community for being greedy and then tell Canadians that "survival of the fittest nations has become the rule of life." The man who invoked the War Measures Act in Quebec brought us the Charter of Rights and Freedoms and spent his last days in office in the pursuit of world peace.[2]

His last days in power were also spent on a binge of patronage unequalled before or since in Canadian politics, although Mulroney came close. If nothing else Trudeau proved that you can fool most of the people most of the time and a large part of them all of the time. He referred to us as the great "unwashed" and was confident that we were collectively stupid enough to believe him no matter what he said. He continually campaigned for programs and policy that he did not pursue when elected or campaigned against other policy proposals of the other parties only to adopt them when elected. The fact that we fell for it repeatedly tends to confirm his suspicions. This is especially true of Ontarians. He knew he could buy the Atlantic Provinces with UI and Economic Development funds that served no purpose other than to buy votes. He knew he could count on Quebec support therefore he only needed Ontario. He got them by deceit and deception. For example, he campaigned against Wage and Price controls then implemented them. He also campaigned against a large increase in gas tax proposed by the conservatives only to implement a bigger one when elected. Another stalwart of liberal campaigning was and is the propensity to use innuendo and suggestion that the other parties will gut and/or eliminate the social programs that Canadians hold so dear. This has become liberal doctrine as we have seen in Chrétien's three red books. They are red for a reason; not just because they are liberal but because they are dangerous.

These very programs that generate dependency reduce productivity and wither the rugged individualism and self-sufficiency that is at the heart of Capitalism, are now considered untouchable, by most Canadians, despite their onerous tax burden. Trudeau blamed the experts for not costing the programs out properly for the excessive costs. He has little to say about the mountain of debt that his government accumulated during his reign. Although he constantly referred to individual freedoms as the heart of liberalism he seems not to realize that his policies impeded the individual freedom that he supposedly held so dear. For example, his governments introduced new taxes and increased old ones to the point where personal income tax skyrocketed. Moreover, EI and CPP premiums were constantly going up. In addition, and even more compelling, was the cost and magnitude of government borrowing which caused the rise in interest rates and crowded out private borrowing while progressively requiring more taxes to be spent on servicing this growing mountain of debt. All the while more of each federal dollar spent went to service this mountain of debt and not one cent to reduce it. All these financial transactions by the government reduced individual freedom by reducing dramatically disposable income. Real disposable income decreased during Trudeau's stewardship resulting in diminished expectations and the replacement of the consumer by government as the King in the economy. This continues today. In today's society, with the exception of ones health, there is no better way to impair individual freedom than to reduce disposable income. So once again, Trudeau said the right things but his actions belied reality.

And yet the great unwashed continue to ask for more social programs not realizing that this will only result in higher taxes. This liberal legacy remains with us today in the form of various proposals in the liberal red books that the great unwashed believe will happen on each new election call. All this proves is that we are indeed sheep ready to be led to slaughter by leaders with sufficient charisma and power to intimidate and overrule basic freedoms and economic reality. The rule of logic and reason that Trudeau insisted on and is credited with escaped his economics every time and we Canadians were left to pick up the tab. His disciple, Chrétien, continues this bankrupt approach to economics.

Finally, it must be said that Trudeau omitted, obscured, obfuscated, revised history and downright lied to achieve his goal of bilingualism. In the introduction to Shaw and Albert's book, "*Partition*", Eugene Forsey, an acknowledged Canadian constitutional expert, sums up the debate on Quebec Independence:

> It is high time someone spoke out loud and clear to challenge the bland, often insolent, assumptions which have been foisted on a gullible public. This book challenges a series of those assumptions.
>
> Second, the debate has too often taken place in a great "cloud of unknowing" fairy-tales. That cloud this book penetrates, those fairy-tales it shows up for the imaginative nonsense they are.[3]

End Notes

1. Barlow and Campbell, "*Straight Through the Heart*," Toronto: HarperCollins, 1996, p. 36.
2. Ibid., p. 37.
3. Lionel Albert and William Shaw, "*Partition: The Price of Quebec's Independence*," Point Claire: Thornhill Publishing, 1980, p. 1.

8

Commercial and Guardian Moral Syndromes

Jane Jacobs in her book "*Systems of Survival*" a dialogue on the Moral Foundations of Commerce and Politics demonstrates, in a thought provoking way, the differences between the morals embodied and practised in commercial and political activities. The reader is left with two opposing methodologies that go a long way to explaining, to the layman, the lack of principle and ethics evident in politics and politicians. This is necessary because most citizens are employed in the business of commerce or trading and although they perceive the dichotomy between commerce and politics they are often unable to understand why the morals of one venture are anathema in the other.

The next page shows a summary of the two for comparison. A quick scan of the two disparate characteristics demonstrates that there are two distinct cultures at work here. The question that immediately emerges when one considers the Guardian or political syndrome is that we should not be surprised by the apparent immoral and unethical conduct of politicians since it is part of their culture. On the other hand, those, or most, of us who work in the business world, in various industries, are more familiar and compatible with the Commercial

Commercial and Guardian Moral Syndromes

Commercial Moral Syndrome	Guardian Moral Syndrome
Shun force	Shun trading
Come to voluntary agreements	Exert prowess
Be honest	Be obedient and disciplined
Collaborate easily with strangers and aliens	Adhere to tradition
Compete	Respect hierarchy
Respect contracts	Be loyal
Use initiative and enterprise	Take vengeance
Be open to inventiveness and novelty	Deceive for the sake of the task
Be efficient	Make rich use of leisure
Promote comfort and convenience	Be ostentatious
Dissent for the sake of the task	Dispense largesse
Invest for productive purposes	Be exclusive
Be industrious	Show fortitude
Be thrifty	Be fatalistic
Be optimistic	Treasure honour[1]

model. To illustrate more adequately the sinister and Machiavellian style of PET it is only necessary to briefly link events surrounding his Prime Ministership with the guardian model. Politicians generally, and PET specifically, do not participate in trading but in zero-sum games. It is winning at any cost or all costs. Inevitably, there must be a loser and that is usually the citizens, the nation, or both. The NEP is the best example wherein PET confronted Alberta and its Premier, Peter Lougheed a reasonable and gentle man, head on in order to bring him and his Province to heal in the turmoil caused by the energy crisis in the mid 70s. Based on false assumptions (oil was no longer nor will ever again be subject to the law of supply and demand) and publicly funded propaganda they met at high noon and the feds prevailed. That Lougheed later partly reversed the biased and flawed policy also demonstrates this brutal intrusion into Provincial rights as laid out in the constitution at the time. Trudeau would secure Canadian or Arabian oil for Quebec and Ontario at the best price and at a great loss to the Alberta treasury. It was an example of his gunslinger tactics based on flawed economic realities. The fact that Western alienation resulted was of no significance to Trudeau at the time but has had a lingering negative effect on Federal Provincial relations ever since. To some it was the clarion call for the Reform party.

Obedience and Discipline are the key to liberal power, especially that of the Prime Minister. They were enforced by Trudeau through his system of rewards and punishments. He also moved quickly to consolidate power in the PMO and over time, with both conservative and liberal governments, this concentration of power has reached extremes. In fact, everyday MPs are now irrelevant to the governing of Canada. "Backbenchers were losers, too. In the words of one, they are "nobodies" in the Chrétien government; their voices have been largely silenced.

Chrétien has reacted strongly against dissenters, threatening that he might refuse to sign their nomination papers in the next election as punishment."[2] Trudeau's use of patronage and cronyism became so extreme that his successor, Turner, could not defend it during election debates with Mulroney and he subsequently lost the election. This was considered the turning point in the election that saw Mulroney and the conservatives win their first majority government. Ironically, it was Mulroney's patronage that helped banish the conservatives later into political oblivion. However, the lesson is that blind trust and conformity is the cornerstone of acquiring and maintaining power that is the lifeblood of socialism. Power, raw power, was the catalyst that made Trudeau tick and he garnered and nurtured every opportunity to exercise it. It is what distinguishes politicians. Professor Hayek is once again instructive when he points out the character of politicians, particularly those who support their leader. He states: "The only tastes which are satisfied are the taste for power as such and the pleasure of being obeyed and of being part of a well-functioning and immensely powerful machine to which everything else must give way."[3] If you tune in to question period on any day you will see this satisfaction on the smug faces of the government benches and hear it in the condescending responses to the questions posed. For analytic purposes let us examine each of the guardian syndrome characteristics in some detail in an effort to expose the limited character that constitutes those who seek politics as a vocation.

One of the characters in Jane Jacobs's book, "*Systems of Survival*" points out the similarity with the guardian syndrome (politics) and the Mafia:

> In any case, the Mafia bears ample marks of guardian moral provenance: Prowess-the Mafia's reliance on physical

force, or threat of it, to get its way. That's why it is so dangerous to cross. Respects for hierarchy — the Mafia 'families' have their soldiers, their capos, or captains, their consiglieres, or councillors, their dons, and in alliances among families, their dons of all dons. The families know as much about loyalty as Machiavelli himself — how to deserve it, buy it, subvert it, terrorize people into it, sniff our disloyalty, penalize it. Execution is the penalty for treason. Omerta, the law of silence, is the law of unconditional loyal mutual support against outsiders. The Mafia venerates tradition and rituals. It is exclusive and inbred. It dispenses largess; that is the 'godfather' side of dons. It thrives on deceit for the sake of its operations. It makes a cult of fortitude. It employs ostentation — shows of conspicuous force or wealth to impress henchmen, rivals, and people it seeks to subvert.[4]

It is not so difficult to draw an analogy between the Mafia organization and function with the various political party systems within Canada. In the federal liberal party, for example, Jean is the Don of Dons, cabinet ministers are the lesser Dons, their consiglieres are in the Prime Ministers Office and Cabinet ministers offices, the Captains are MPs, and the soldiers are their riding associations. You can see that the Mafia bears a striking resemblance to the political parties at work in this country. Let's examine it a little more closely. In the following analysis you will find a comparison between organized crime and politics at the end of each section except where it is so obvious there is no need to elaborate.

End Notes

1. Jane Jacobs, "*Systems of Survival,*" Toronto: Random House of Canada, 1994, p. Appendix.
2. Barlow and Campbell, "*Straight Through the Heart,*" Toronto: HarperCollins, 1996, p. 135.
3. Hayek, "*The Road to Serfdom,*" Chicago: University of Chicago Press, 1994, p. 166.
4. Jacobs, "*Systems of Survival,*" p. 94.

9

Trading

Politics, the art of the possible, would be better served if politicians were predisposed to give and take rather than just take. The mindset is one of zero-sum strategies rather than win-win ones. Trudeau writes negatively about the decades of attempts to repatriate and amend the constitution. As you might expect he attacked the Provinces for their intransigence and their demand for concessions at every turn and at every new meeting. Trudeau had a sound basis for criticizing the Provinces; particularly Quebec who's Premiers reneged on two different attempts to agree on an amending formula. He accepted the flawed Charter of Rights with its "notwithstanding" clause as a victim to allow progressing the file. All in all he went ahead because this action was to be his legacy and it truly is despite its flaws, ignoring, of course, that it is merely and extension of Diefenbaker's 1961 Bill of Rights. In fact, it is a lesser document because of a major error or a major achievement. The major error/achievement in the Charter of Rights and Freedoms comes in article 15, equality rights. Sub-para b that specifically allows governments to discriminate for reasons of race, national or ethnic origin, colour, religion, sex, age or mental or physical disability while prohibiting citizens from doing so. This is unjust since no one, including governments, should be permitted to discriminate. It is however, the basis, for biculturalism, affirmative action, minority and visible minority preference, social engineering, and other injustices, no doubt, yet to come. This is why I am inclined to see it as a Trudeau achievement as he was aware that Quebec would use this provision to limit language rights in Quebec. Combined with its own immigration policy, thanks to the opting out provision of the constitution and its own tax and pension policies, this provision constitutes a method for Quebec to continue to build its "national stature" in the eyes of Quebecers, not to mention its census figures. For conspiracy nuts one could easily conclude that Trudeau allowed the opting out and notwithstanding clauses to remain because he wanted Quebec to have a way out if his grand plan A should fail. Plan B would then be easier to achieve. Just for a moment think of what would happen to Canada if the other Provinces started to follow Quebec's lead in extricating itself from Canada. How long would these provisions last if they started to opt out of national programs without financial penalty? For Quebec it is a simple method of financing her cultural imperatives at others expense and Trudeau knew it. This makes him a party to institutionalized treason as the only outcome could be the break-up of Canada and all the perceived wrongs would have been repaid and Quebec would be free and independent. In his critical review of Socialism Professor Hayek informs us that once we have taken the initial steps towards discrimination the next ones get easier since the basis has already been imprinted on the minds of both those who discriminate and those who are victims. "Discrimination between members and non-members of closed groups, not to speak of nationals of different countries, is accepted more and more as a matter of course; injustices inflicted on individuals by government action in the interest of a group are disregarded with an indifference hardly distinguishable from callousness; ... liberals."[1] For the socialists in Ottawa and in Trudeau's cabinet it just became easier and easier to jam it up the English and with each opting out Quebecers become more and more a closed group.

Similarly in the financial realm, the government accounts in their own magic slight of hand manner while prohibiting others from similar activity. The recently dethroned federal Finance Minister, Paul Martin, is famous for his accounting finesse to the point where a budget isn't necessary anymore. Nonetheless, it is patently wrong for the government to hold its citizens to one methodology while it conforms to another. The first law should be that everyone, including governments must conform to all the laws of Canada. Otherwise there is not equality before the law as is so often asserted.

It is a paradox that trading, which is the lifeblood of the Canadian economy, is anathema to politicians and political parties. Yet, it prevails in the day to day work between departments and governments at various levels. Perhaps it is the preponderance of lawyers or the utilization of lawyers in the system that is raised on the art and science of confrontation. As one who worked in the bureaucracy for 36 years I am very familiar with the power that the legal profession and the law have over political action or inaction. What has always amazed me was the reluctance to change laws, legislation, or regulations that did not envision the kinds of problems that imminent change brings on. Known as red tape it is the single most important element in the obstruction of bureaucratic progress. The Charter, Trudeau's legacy, is an everyday legal event now with the courts endeavouring to interpret it. It has created much work for lawyers and unfortunately has shifted the making of laws from Parliament to the Courts, an eventuality that was neither desired nor intended.

To further illustrate the aversion that politicians have to trading it should be noted that the subsequent majority conservative governments wasted years and billions on attempting to achieve Quebec's agreement on the constitution. Countless conferences resulted in the Meech Lake accord, an agreement made behind closed doors but eventually rejected. Thanks to Elijah Harper and the Newfoundland legislature this all party agreement time lapsed. A second attempt, the Charlottown accord, another all party agreement, went down to defeat at the hands of the citizens of Canada. It was fitting that this agreement was subjected to a referendum since it would affect all Canadians. It was also fitting that by rejecting it overwhelmingly the citizens were made aware that their politicians were not in fact representing their interests. This direct participation in passing a law has not been repeated as politicians are not inclined to subject their attempts to horse trade or impose their will to the ratification of the public. These two attempts at constitutional reform were of course Mulroney's attempt to upstage Trudeau who had succeeded where others had failed, albeit by taking unilateral action, albeit with Supreme Court approval. The persistence and insistence of repatriating the constitution including a Charter of Rights and Freedoms was another example of Trudeau's willingness to "tough it out" despite the opposition, and there was a lot.

Trudeau later rose to take on the Mulroney government over the Meech Lake Accord and the Charlottetown accord essentially for two reasons. First, he believed that both would reduce the power of the central government and that they would water down the Charter of Rights. In addition, this action would usurp his legacy so it is not surprising that he was against both. In his 1 October 1992 speech to the Cité Liberte dinner, which was televised, he responds to a question regarding his selective use of the "Notwithstanding" clause in the Charter. Bear in mind that he always maintained that the notwithstanding clause was a flaw that he had to accept in order to get agreement on the Charter being included in the Constitution. He replied in part that "the citizen pays his taxes, and obeys the laws. So the collectivity has rights. It's just that according to my philosophy, according to liberal philosophy and the philosophy of the Enlightenment, the collectivity always has rights delegated to it by the individual. The collectivity is not the bearer of rights: it receives the rights it exercises from the citizens." The use of the term collectivity as opposed to community is a clue to where this view originates.

This is an important point. What he is saying is that you have the right to alter collectivity rights through your participation in the electoral process. Unfortunately, as fewer and fewer voters exercise this right it plays into the hands of politicians particularly the socialists who have managed to balkanize the country into the East (the Maritime provinces), the West (Manitoba westward), the Best (Ontario and Quebec) and the Rest (Territories). As long as citizens refuse to vote they are essentially giving governments a carte blanche with regard to the abuse of individual rights. It is also curious that the notwithstanding clause gave Trudeau and his government the right to discriminate against Canadians in the public service by using race as the prime criteria for advancement over merit. In this sense a specific group, a minority, was given preference. Later the Trudeau government would experiment with other groups in social engineering within the military, the RCMP, and the public service. Even today it still goes on. Moreover, it is so endemic and systematic now that the sheer weight of numbers will likely thwart any attempt to restore the merit principle to primacy. Notwithstanding what I have said about the Meech Lake and Charlottetown accords,

Trudeau was correct in his analysis of their flaws. But the one thing that needs to be done is the removal of the notwithstanding clause from the Charter so that no one can discriminate against others, including the governments. Just ask yourself, who says the public service or the army must reflect the broader population? Why should people have to do things that they do not necessarily want to do? And why should others be denied the opportunity they are qualified for and want to do? Why does the government have the right to restrict you from a position you are qualified for because it wants to attract another lesser qualified one because of skin colour or some other irrelevant characteristic? I, for one, do not accept that my government should be allowed to do things that it specifically denies of others.

When the constitution is next amended there are a couple of points that need to be changed in order to affect provincial equality. They are first to eliminate the guarantee of a certain number of MPs from Quebec despite the fact that their population does not warrant them. All the other provinces are governed by representation by population and so should Quebec. Also, Quebec should not be entitled to three Supreme Court judges but also a number commensurate with her population. And who said that Quebec doesn't have special status?

Like the French, Quebecers need to be different, it is a cultural imperative. But they are also presumptive without the underlying proof. They say they speak French but Quebecois is in fact a dialect. Many bureaucrats found this out in language training when having succeeded in becoming bilingual they could not communicate with the Quebecers. And this way of referring to themselves, as Quebecois, was adopted from the traditional "Canadien" when the PQ evolved from the Quebec liberal party in order to distance them from this historical proud reference. They abolished the legislative assembly for a national assembly and renamed the Premier, the Prime-Minister. They fly a former flag of a monarchy that is now a republic. And they are currently spending a lot of money in coming up with new French words for English ones. And who knows, one of these days they may see the wisdom of turning right on a red.

Finally, you don't trade with the Mafia, they take and you willingly comply or face the consequences. It sounds very much like taxes.

End Notes

1. Hayek, "*The Road to Serfdom*," Chicago: University of Chicago Press, 1994, p. 234.

10

Exert Prowess

Trudeau himself demonstrated this quality better than anyone before or since in Canadian politics. He was never unsure of himself, convinced he was right in all matters, and willing to contest anyone else's views. He described his encounters with other heads of governments in *"Memoirs"* and hastened to tell us that he was never bested by any of them. To his credit, he demonstrated that he was a sound judge of character insofar as the individuals he sparred verbally with but he also demonstrated his preference for socialist thinking and those who practised it. He was more than a worthy opponent which explains why he steadfastly defended his policies even though many of them were wrong. It is unfortunate that the political system could not find a worthy opponent during his tenure as it might have prevented some of the colossal waste and the enduring debt that Canadians must bear for generations to come.

Trudeau did not shy away from interfering in Provincial matters where it might aid his goal. Readers will remember that he was turned down by Bill Davis on his request to make Ontario officially bilingual. He campaigned openly and financed groups in Manitoba in order to have official bilingualism approved there. He was actively opposed by Sterling Lyon and the conservatives. One of his own cabinet members, James Richardson, resigned from the federal government and aided the fight against bilingualism in Manitoba. He is quoted as follows in Russell Doern's book, "*The Battle Over Bilingualism*":

> Unfortunately, the Manitoba Government is making the same mistake, that so many others have made, of believing that bilingualism is a uniting force. Canadians have been told by Prime Minister Trudeau and others for the past 15 years that the way to save Canada, the way to unite Canada, is to promote bilingualism throughout Canada.
>
> The truth is that legislated and enforced bilingualism has never been a unifying force and it never can be. Official bilingualism at the Federal level is not uniting Canada, it is dividing Canada-and now, the same misguided thinking is disrupting the harmony and mutual respect and goodwill towards each other that has always characterized Manitobans.[1]

In the Mafia no one questions the Don. It is like in the military or the corporate world where there are two rules. Rule one is that the boss is always right. Rule two is that when the boss is wrong, revert to rule one.

End Notes

1. Russell Doern, "*The Battle over Bilingualism*," Winnipeg: Cambridge Publishers, 1985, p. 187.

11

Be Obedient and Disciplined

It is a well established fact that the glue that melds any political party comes from a united front and there is a preponderance of examples where those who were obedient and disciplined remained and were rewarded while those who did not, were not. Trudeau brooked no dissent from the Cabinet view which he controlled closely. His use of closure and lack of free votes in Parliament effectively reduced it to a moribund institution. His control of the Senate was absolute and he filled it with loyalists. His appointments to the thousands of positions in government and government agencies secured the liberal hold and his social engineering in the public service ensured compliance with liberal ideology. This too remains today and if anything has progressed to the theatre of the absurd as evidenced by the Senate revolt when Mulroney appointed enough conservative senators to control the Senate. If nothing else it demonstrated the power of appointment and this should be fixed in the public mind. Other changes to the Senate have rendered it from being a "second sober thought" to being a "last gasp before capitulation to the House". In this way Trudeau further centralized decision making to the inner cabinet to the exclusion of all else.

Failure to obey and remain subordinate results in a fitting for concrete boots in organized crime. In politics, it usually results in a golden handshake in the form of a plum position. Either way, you are out.

12

Tradition

A frontal assault on one of Canada's proud and capable institutions was undertaken by allowing Paul Hellyer to raise hell with the military. Although this was initiated by Pearson, Trudeau supported Hellyer's demolition. The liberals unceremoniously removed the Royal from the Navy and the Air Force along with most of their fighting power. They integrated and then unified the armed forces and through successive budget cuts eliminated the "armed" from the forces. The once proud services became eunuchs of the UN. They still are! Trudeau, it appears, would stop at nothing to remove the true stamp of British heritage from Canada while ameliorating the French one. The military now conforms to his pacifist way of thinking not because they don't have the heart to fight but because they have been deprived of the hardware, training, and support to do so. As a consequence we find ourselves dependant on another country for our security. We have methodically replaced our warriors with peacekeepers and they are totally different things. That is why the Americans retrain every peacekeeper back into a warrior when they return from UN duties. All the while our governments have grieved about our loss of sovereignty but what is sovereignty without your own security? Again, Trudeau and his followers have talked the talk but failed to walk. Today in the middle of a terrorist war we are extremely vulnerable with no further commitment to increased security. We do not deserve sovereignty! Also, we should remind ourselves that as Machiavelli said that if you put your security in the hands of your friend you may find that you have another enemy. Until Trudeau we had the democratic tradition of providing our own security and since we have shunned this requisite of nationhood. Chrétien and his government have merely exasperated an already deplorable situation and the military continues to erode by exodus and malignant neglect.

His assault on Parliament also changed the operation of that institution to the point of rendering it less and less relevant to governance. The wanton use of closure in order to reduce debate moved from a rarity to a common usage as one example. Also, his propensity to govern by orders-in-council essentially bypassed Parliament.

Trudeau endeavoured to alter our relationship with the Commonwealth by slowly withdrawing support while increasing our activity in the Francophonie, an association of French speaking States, primarily in Africa. Now we see more concentration and spending on Francophonie activities than on Commonwealth ones. Trudeau did this in order to focus Canadian attention on our French roots as opposed to our English ones. Once again, it has become a way to pipeline federal tax dollars to Quebec and Quebecers. Meanwhile the financial treatment of our Commonwealth and Olympic athletes is woefully inadequate.

Everyone is familiar with the code of silence of organized crime. Likewise, it is next to impossible to find the truth when dealing with government even with access to information laws and other feeble avenues especially when the government itself actively fights their own laws.

13

Respect Hierarchy

Little needs to be said here. It is clear, to most everyone, that the party system in effect controls Canadian politics and is based on party disciple and respecting the hierarchy. That hierarchy starts with the individual party member then proceeds upward through the riding association, MP, party caucus, parliamentary secretaries, cabinet ministers, Senators, PMO, and eventually to the PM. The GG is a mere figurehead, although an expensive one. Likewise the Senate and Senators are window dressing but a good place to reward those who have respected the hierarchy. One must bear in mind that this is not a hierarchy of power because the unelected PMO, for example, has more power than cabinet ministers. Recently, we are seeing a small resurgence by lowly MPs seeking to exert more influence over the system. This is in evidence within all but one party who are currently (2002) seeking to replace their leaders. One has resigned, two have verbally said they will leave and one will likely be thrown out. Even a serving PM elected to a majority is on the way out. Perhaps there is hope???

The most interesting aspect of this pecking order of power is that the group closest to the PM, the PMO, is composed of heavy hitters and advisers who are unelected but surpass the influence and power of cabinet ministers and senators. Most MPs won't open their mouths without PMO approval. This puts the PM and his Office in a unique position of being a virtual dictatorship in charge of a nominal democracy. The current PM has stated it many times in many different ways but it always is translated as "I am in charge". This is true and it is wrong! Canadians did not elect 301 members to the House of Commons so that one man, a man selected by the party, can rule. This is in effect the result of our skewed and ineffective electoral system.

To buttress and support the party within the bureaucracy the government ensures that friends and relatives of MPs and Senators, party officials, party loyalists, and those owed favours, are taken in to the public service. And they are taken in at the highest levels even though they often have no experience whatsoever in the department or government. Likewise, Directorships, Chairmanships of Boards, Board members, citizen judges, and countless other positions of authority are lavished on the party faithful. These pseudo-executives are ardent supporters of government policy and essentially beneficiaries of largess. It is an incestuous system that breeds party influence within a supposed apolitical system. This in effect constitutes a false hierarchy of ability and authority based on favouritism. This method of leapfrogging party faithful over the qualified and capable leads to ineffectiveness and low morale in the public service, a chronic problem in the public service, RCMP, and military today. And yet it is accepted by the Canadian public as just another normal perk enjoyed by the party faithful. It must be stopped.

Likewise, the offspring of those in power expect to receive appointments or positions as a matter of their due. Hence, we see the sons and daughters of politicians following in their elders footsteps even though many of them have no experience whatsoever. Today you can see a Trudeau, a Mulroney, or a Clark offspring being groomed by the party to take their rightful place in the political structure. All they have to do is accept the overture and the party will ensure that a Commons seat is bestowed. As a consequence you have young individuals assuming high office untested by the real world and already possessed by the guardian moral syndrome. They are takers. This type of turnover ensures that new ideas and approaches will remain anathema by both the political elite and the politicized bureaucracy. The party has become the sovereign in Canadian politics!

We the electorate only select the MPs. After that the party takes over. The party, using different procedures for different parties, select the leader. The leader of the party with the most MPs becomes the Prime Minister. Once sworn in he or she selects, the agenda, the parliamentary committee chairpersons, the Cabinet and parliamentary secretaries, officials in the PMO, Senators when vacancies arise, the Governor General if required, Supreme Court Judges when vacancies occur, and thousands of Officials required by the various agencies and Crown corporations etc., that support government operations. None of them are elected and unless a Prime Minister goes too far or is incompetent, as in the current case, they serve their full term unless of course the PM calls an election or resigns. This system constitutes a democracy in form only, in essence it is a system of one man/woman government or dictatorship, however benevolent.

I am not a proponent of the US form of government but I do like the idea of government appointees having to be confirmed as well as elected senators and judges. This at least ensures experience and qualifications for the job selected. It also serves as a check on patronage which is scandalous in Canadian politics.

It seems that when citizens realize their limited power

they find it exceedingly easy to withdraw their participation in the process. Concurrently, their withdrawal makes it even easier for the party to subvert the system, such as it is. As we have seen Canadians are abandoning the polls on election day and we will soon be faced with a collapse of efficacy on the part of government. This drives regions and Provinces towards independence or towards our friendly neighbour to the South. Already thousands of Canadians are voting for this solution with their feet. This crisis in government is fast approaching and we simply must modify our political system or it will collapse.

To understand more fully the impact of our party on our political system, I recommend the book *"On the Take: Crime, Corruption and Greed in the Mulroney Years"* by Stevie Cameron. This detailed account reveals the depth and breath of party and politicians' contempt for Canada and her people. More importantly, it demonstrates that this attitude and activity exists in the two major historical parties in Canada.

14

Loyalty

In Trudeau's government and associations you were either loyal or you were out. He was intolerant of criticism and maintained an air of invincibility. He balked at Europe's response to his plans to cut back on NATO and he balked at their lack of response to his "third option", his plan to increase trade with Europe at the expense of the US. He was a constant source of critique and irritation to the US administrations; regardless of their desires Trudeau was always willing to thwart them. His visits to Cuba and his support of Castro combined with his recognition of China severely aggravated Canada/US relations. The infamous President Nixon was less than gratuitous in his appraisal of Trudeau. Likewise Trudeau found him intellectually wanting and unable to fully grasp ideological and historical imperatives. JE Hoover and the FBI built and maintained a file on Trudeau regarding his socialist propensity. The RCMP and the Canadian Military also had a file on Trudeau's activities and associations prior to his rise to political prominence but they were subsequently destroyed, by order. Ironically, this apparent disloyalty to democracy and the western way was counterbalanced by his demand for loyalty from his followers. Those who remained loyal to Trudeau were rewarded with a Senate seat or seat on a board of an agency or similar position where the main requisite was to keep breathing and show up occasionally. Senator Kirby, a Trudeau staffer was appointed to the Senate in his early thirties. I submit that no one at that tender and inexperienced age is worthy of such a post. Nobody had heard much about him until the appointment and there has been little noted since. One wonders what he did for Canada that merited such a plum. Similarly, Michael Pitfield, Trudeau's friend and clerk of the Privy Council, was appointed to the Senate after being fired by Joe Clark. The list is endless.

A recent National Post editorial, entitled "Senate on siesta" published Sep 20, 2002 criticized the Senate for reducing its setting days in this coming session to 87 days, but indicated that the real number would be closer to 69. Senator Sharon Carstairs, liberal *party* leader in the Senate, responded harshly in a letter to the editor, published on 23 Sep 2002, by defending the heavy burden of work that the Senate has to endure. Right! You might remember her as the Liberal Party Leader in Opposition in the Manitoba Legislature way back when; but then again probably not. This form of patronage was honed to a fine art by Trudeau. His last act before thankfully leaving politics was to engage in an orgy of appointments that was so disgusting that it cost his replacement and his rival, Turner, the next election when he could not substantiate it to taxpayers during a debate with Mulroney. Thus, Turner received the back of Trudeau's hand as a parting shot.

15

Vengeance

Trudeau was a master at the subtle art of vengeance; most Machiavellians are. Apart from ensuring a limited time for Turner as party leader through active campaigning for his disciple Chrétien, he made it almost impossible for Turner to defend the actions of the liberal party. Not only was Trudeau opposed to Turner as party leader and PM for political reasons, Turner was not from Quebec and Trudeau was willing to see the liberals defeated if another party leader from Quebec was elected, such as Brian Mulroney. Trudeau's spurning of Turner did not go unnoticed in Quebec and Quebecers voted overwhelmingly for the Conservatives.

The wrath of Trudeau has already been examined in the case of the Alberta and the NEP as well as the overkill in relation to the FLQ crisis. His lack of respect and deep-seated antagonism towards the Monarchy was witnessed in his appointment of primarily French Canadians to the Governor-General position. He struck down the traditions of the military, made wholesale changes in Parliamentary procedures, and substituted a new system of honours and awards thus snubbing the British. Canadians who proudly wore them also took exception and many returned their medals in protest. On the one hand citizens might have perceived his actions as forcing the country to come of age but his actions were never substantiated in that vein, rather they almost always appeared to slight the Monarchy. His pirouette behind the Queen at a state function indicated a rebuke of the Crown rather than a sense of humour and as his principle secretary at the time, Jim Coutts said, it was deliberate and planned. All of Trudeau's actions were deliberate and calculated as in keeping with his character. His sense of self was without limit and he was willing to confront any and all who challenged him. His rebuttal to President Nixon's comments that "he had been called worse things by better people" confirmed his contempt for Nixon and America.

When the Europeans snubbed Trudeau's overtures for more trade in order to diminish American economic influence on Canada, the Europeans countered with a request for a larger contribution to the North Atlantic Treaty Organization (NATO). Trudeau had already started to cut back forces in Europe and his response was to increase and accelerate their withdrawal as well as removing the Nuclear Strike capability from Canadian Forces stationed there which was the only credible part of our presence.

Trudeau travelled to many communist countries and seemed to revel in the shadow of Castro. His trips to Cuba did not go unnoticed in Washington and his mission to China was hotly contested in Washington as well as by some European countries. He seemed to take pleasure in challenging the United States (US) on its foreign policy particularly in Asia and the Middle East. In fairness, there was much to challenge as time has shown but it was more the manner than the substance that upset the US.

The streets have been littered with crime lord vengeance and likewise the political landscape is littered with political enemies.

16

Trudeau/Levesque Conspiracy — Deception

Richard Gwyn wrote that Trudeau was born into two cultures, and born rich. Rene Levesque was not. Yet their two views of where Quebec should fit in Canada came to dominate the political landscape from the early 60's until Levesque's and Trudeau's deaths. Their friendship sealed in early confrereship waned over the years but their mutual respect never did. They held different views and each struggled in their own way to win. Neither did completely. Nevertheless, their quest for the hearts of Quebecers, not Canadians, drove them unwittingly into a conspiracy against the rest of Canada. In those two decades of pitched battles only Quebec and many Quebecers won. Levesque's eventual mission after leaving the Quebec liberal party was to separate from Canada and form a French State; Trudeau's mission, much grander in scope and devious in execution, befitting a man of his higher intellect and cunning, was to deliver Canada to Quebec and make Canada a French State.

Sun Tzu wrote: "All warfare is based on deception."[1] A reasonable person might conclude on the basis of facts that Trudeau entered federal politics along with some of his closest allies in order to execute a takeover of the federal government in order to recast Canada as a socialist state rather than a democratic one. David Somerville outlined much of Trudeau's youth and exposure to socialist doctrine in his book *"Trudeau Revealed by his Actions and Words"*. He came to Ottawa to change history. No longer would the French be losers but they would control the country or leave it and establish a Republic much like mother France. Plan A was to appease Quebec within the federation and if that failed Plan B would be to secede. Plan A was Trudeau's; Plan B later became Levesque's.

Lester Pearson was the PM at the time Trudeau, Marchand, and Pelletier came to Ottawa and Trudeau very quickly became Pearson's Parliamentary Secretary in 1966. They were of like mind as they had both studied at the London School of Economics under Professor Laski, a known socialist. Pearson was infatuated with Trudeau, a fellow socialist, but one would like to think unaware of Trudeau's plan. Pearson went on to put Trudeau, Marchand, Pelletier, and Chrétien in cabinet. Trudeau would later appoint Lalonde. In 1968 Pearson retired and Trudeau won the leadership of the Liberal Party. Trudeau was Pearson's choice as a successor.

It is clear from the party Trudeau helped form in 1954, Le Rassemblement (gathering, union), that along with his associates, Levesque, Pepin, Pelletier, Marchand, Bourassa and many others that they entered into an unstated conspiracy to wrest control of the federal government. Some would go to Ottawa and others would stay in Quebec in order to exercise power in both camps. The departure from the Quebec Liberals and the formation of the Parti Quebecois (PQ) by Levesque led the Quebec faction to seek secession. Trudeau was by now committed to maintaining power and countering the Quebec nationalists. Those who knew Trudeau's character could have predicted this fight between patriots fought on the grand scale of Canada. It was the Plains of Abraham all over again but fought by the French only. Until the second referendum Canadians, outside of Quebec, were mere spectators. Thankfully, the rest of Canada has been sensitized and now any question of secession will be determined by them, not just Quebecers. In character, Trudeau later helped to scotch the Meech and Charlottetown accords in keeping with his rigid views on Quebec Nationalism and his determination to bury the Quebec Nationalists while preserving his legacy.

Some proof of the conspiracy is contained in Richard Gwyn's book "*The Northern Magus*" where he quotes Jean Luc Pepin, then the minister of Industry, Trade and Commerce, "I cannot swear it, but I think we are thinking ourselves. We ourselves were a small group, Trudeau, Pelletier, Marchand, Lalonde, Chrétien, Myself, and a few people in the Civil Service, say 50 all told ... we were bringing off a revolution. We held the key posts. We were making the civil service bilingual, kicking and screaming all the time. We were a well organized group of revolutionaries."[2] Clearly Plan A was put in effect immediately that Trudeau became PM and all ran smoothly until Levesque, initially a Trudeau ally, reneged. No doubt it was a clash of egos that caused the rift in the conspirators. By this time many of them had served their purpose and gone on to their patronage rewards. Nonetheless, neither Trudeau nor Levesque was about to capitulate. Levesque and his new entourage in Quebec wanted Plan B while Trudeau was committed to Plan A. Chrétien, a key player in Trudeau's plan was waiting in the wings to continue Plan A after Turner was relieved of the leadership. Trudeau's orgy of patronage on retirement ensured that Turner would lose to Mulroney. This would give the liberals a chance to renew themselves while the conservatives shot themselves in the foot trying to cope with the financial mess that the liberal party left behind.

It was fortunate for Canadians that Levesque refused to agree with an amending formula initially and later refused to sign the proposed constitution. This scuttled a guaranteed veto by Quebec over constitutional amendments. When Mulroney became PM he took on the task of reaching an "entent" through the Meech Lake Accord initially and then through the Charlottetown Accord. This was significant for two reasons. First, thanks to Manitoba MLA Harper and the Newfoundland Legislature Meech time expired. It would have given Quebec special status and a veto along with many other benefits. Second, and thankfully the last attempt by Mulroney, the Charlottetown Accord was to be ratified by the people, an innovative concept. Again, Quebec would have been the main beneficiary but it was soundly voted down by the citizens of Canada. It is in this sense that neither Trudeau nor Levesque prevailed.

This was a victory of sorts for the PQ who now could concentrate on separatism and creating the Republic of Quebec in North America. But it was a real victory for Canadians who demonstrated that by now our supposed system of Representative Government was kaput. The people had rejected, soundly, the accord that was endorsed by all political parties. This made it clear that the people and the polity were on different song sheets. Effectively, the ad nausea constitutional arguments and attempts at resolution would be put on the back burner. But, Trudeau's constitution and Charter of Rights and Freedoms remained. Many consider them to be an achievement suitable for a God but as has been demonstrated they are seriously flawed. Nonetheless, Trudeau had taken another step in breaking the link to Mother England and given the French a stronger position in Canada. This also marked the decline and eventual fall of the Conservatives from power and the emergence of Chrétien and the liberals to continue the work of Trudeau on Plan A. The federal conservatives still wonder what happened to their party but it is abundantly clear that by submitting to Trudeau's B&B plans and his constitutional proposals that they were in effect no different than liberals. They let their party faithful down and have suffered accordingly.

That Trudeau deceived the Canadian people is without doubt. He came to Ottawa to change Canada and he did. However, he did not change it in the way most Canadians thought or would want. He brought his socialist baggage and his cultural bias along with him and was determined that he would right the long list of wrongs perpetrated on Quebec by the rest of Canada. In that, he was guilty of a great deception and he succeeded, to the degree he did, by deluding most Canadians. But it doesn't end there.

In order to incapacitate the enemy and render him ineffective before battle requires intelligence. "Thus, what enables the wise sovereign and the good general to strike and conquer, and achieve things beyond the reach of ordinary men, is foreknowledge. ... Hence the use of spies, ..."[3] Trudeau was a student of history and a wanderer in countries known for revolution and he met with men who had some success with forced change. He knew that in order to effect change or revision there is often bloodshed. Therefore, it is neither surprising nor unexpected that he would attempt to render any individual or institution ineffective should it become necessary to resort to violence. As a consequence of his pacifist views and his knowledge of the past, he sought to render some of the country's tools against sedition useless should it become necessary. That is why it was necessary for B&B to be so quickly implemented and for Quebecers to take control over the departments and agencies that might interfere with Trudeau's plans. That the military was integrated with the department of national defence and soon thereafter unified served to throw it into complete turmoil and confusion, where it remains today, thus allowing the infusion of francophones at all levels and in all types of employ to proceed apace. Attendant to this was the determined withdrawal of funds through successive budget cuts and the tangential rundown of firepower of the forces. Later, as we have seen, refinements such as French language units and basing plans have effectively balanced the military within and without Quebec. Also, all the Canadian Forces are now staffed with sufficient French representation that any attempt to use them effectively to forestall or preclude separation or independence for Quebec would be thwarted.

Loyalty to Canada in much of the military cannot be assured and this was demonstrated by Lucien Bouchard on the eve of the last referendum when he wrote to many Officers in the Canadian Forces to determine their allegiance. Unfortunately, no one followed up this subversion so it is not know what luck he may have achieved but the fact that he attempted to test certain military members is telling. Similarly, with other departments and the RCMP, it is not assured that they would be useful instruments in a situation where Quebec might come in conflict with Canada over separation or independence. In any event, Trudeau's cunning use of biculturalism has given some degree of comfort to the nationalists within Quebec that if push came to shove, much of the federal organization and infrastructure could be sabotaged. That remains the situation today and makes Canada very vulnerable to determined separatists within and makes our neighbour to the south uneasy as well. It is doubtful that the United States would set idly by and allow Canada to dismember without taking measures to protect her strategic and domestic interests. Only a fool would conclude that they do not have plans to do so. As Trudeau was aware, the fate of Canada does not rest solely in the hands of Canadians.

End Notes

1. Phillips, "*Roots of Strategy*," Mechanicsburg: Stackpole Books, 1985, p. 18.
2. Richard Gwyn, "*The Northern Magus*," Toronto: PaperJacks, 1981, p. 135.
3. Phillips, "*Roots of Strategy*," Mechanicsburg: Stackpole Books, 1985, pp. 60–61.

17

Leisure

Politicians have to make good use of leisure because through their management of government and organization they spend a significant amount of time away from Parliament. There are many reasons for this but primarily with regard to Trudeau it was much easier to rule by edict in the form of or orders-in-council. By effectively and constantly subverting the role of Parliament Trudeau brought the real power into the Cabinet and the PMO. However, he had to continue with the illusion that Parliament was working so that the people would not be alarmed by his pursuit of power and the neutering of Parliament. Moreover, with the use of closure less time was and is required in Parliament. This left ample time to travel, ostensibly on government business, to various conferences around the world, state visits, vacations, fact-finding missions, provincial and municipal visits, disaster area visitations and countless other reasons. Political meetings, party gatherings, conventions, social events, and state dinners and the like are all events conducted more leisurely than parliamentary proceedings and cabinet committee meetings.

Trudeau expanded the cabinet and the number of government departments as well as his advisors and staffers in order to allow more time to himself so that he could reflect on the issues of the day and Canada's place in the changing world. Also, he was constantly required to create new opportunities for Quebec and Quebecers within Canada. He was a great patron of the arts and used taxpayer's money lavishly on this cultural segment. He ensured objects of art were part of every federal building; he oversaw the creation of the NAC, National Gallery, and ensured that there were generous grants for writers, artists, theatre, and entertainers whose efforts were spent on the Canadian elite but paid for by the Canadian unwashed. The real talent goes elsewhere or manages to market their wares without state sponsorship. Thus, we see many Canadian entertainers, broadcasters, athletes, and actors in the US where real talent is allowed to mature unlike the CBC wannabes.

Trudeau, in his usual indignant way, took great pride in supporting the arts and ensuring that Canadians were exposed to the works of the NFB and other icons of Canada such as the CBC, especially Radio-Canada, the French network. He encouraged the setup of French networks in other parts of Canada as well despite the population numbers all at taxpayer expense. Of course, the media idolized him and ensured that his view was given prominence and support. So what if it required public support in order to survive! Socialists, after all, are not inclined to compete and in Trudeau's time, as today, there is no longer a need for a national network but governments are reluctant to give up a well oiled propaganda machine. Likewise, those in the CBC are most reluctant to have to go to work.

Members of crime families do not work; that is for lesser folk. Similarly, politicians pretend to work but the real work is done by the public service. The politicians plan how they will spend your money. The mafia plan how they will steal your money.

18

Ostentatious

Most everything that Trudeau touched was characterized by size and style. Mirabel, which will be discussed later, is a monument to the scope of Trudeau's adventures. It is also testimony to the mountain of debt he created. His support for the arts and artists is legendary and sorely missed but there are some good examples that ascribe his flair. In Ottawa alone there is the NAC, the National Gallery, the External Affairs edifice, the government buildings in Hull, and the "objets d' art" that adorned them as well as the countless sculptures that mark the entrance to many government buildings. However, one of his most beloved projects was the restoration of Louisburg. As the first French outpost in Canada it required special attention in order to elaborate and raise the French Fact and the two Nation concept of Canada. The reconstruction took years and countless dollars to re-establish what was once destroyed by the British. This expense was justified in the name of tourism and French pride but in reality it was just another in a long list of slights at "Les Anglais". The art adoring government buildings and inside as well, ordered by Trudeau, turned out to be controversial but was a great boost to artists in Canada and was probably purchased at exorbitant costs. In Trudeau's first term any project that would elevate French and/or denigrate English was fair game and the backlash almost cost him the next election.

Both crime bosses and political bosses travel first class through life until their number is up.

19

Largess

The prize for largess, in the form of taxpayer's money goes to a certain Cabinet Minister from Cape Breton who systematically over decades managed to squander billions into the coal mines and steel mills of Cape Breton. He unabashedly pumped funds into these relics of the war producing low quality steel and coal. The steel was destined to Canadian companies such as CN and CP for low quality rails while better quality at a lower cost could have been imported from Japan; CN had no choice since it was government owned. The coal was consumed to create more pollution than was necessary. However, jobs were maintained and a seat in Parliament was guaranteed. Eventually this MP won the Atlantic lottery and was awarded a seat in the Senate; a reward second only to a seat on the Board of Directors of Mirabel. The mines and factories are still costing Canadians although it is mostly Provincial funds. The Senator, now retired, has been provided with an office in Ottawa at taxpayers expense, for the past six years, in order to write his memoirs. This demonstrates, once again, politicos inability to remove their snouts from the public trough once they have become addicted to the swill.

Mirabel International Airport stands out as a true

Trudeau boondoggle that seems to have escaped public scrutiny despite its continuing uselessness. Ostensibly built to rival Toronto as the hub of international air travel in Canada, it was built long before the traffic warranted it and has been mostly idle ever since. The cost to expropriate Quebec Farmers and the turmoil that created aside, it was clearly an unnecessary airport. Add to the billions it cost to construct, by the same companies that built the big "O" and all the graft thereto, the fact that it has lost approximately a cool million a month since completion and you can see that it warrants honourable mention as an icon to central planning and largess. It has been a repository for failed Quebec politicos and bag men who have been rewarded far beyond their worth. Still the airport of the future awaits one. Instead of looking for a mountain to rename after Trudeau the government should name this mountain of debt and deficit after him. The HRDC waste pales in comparison to this forgotten sink hole for taxpayer dollars.

While Trudeau was in power huge office buildings sprung up in Hull and the Ottawa-Hull name began to appear where Ottawa usually did. He transferred whole departments of government to Hull in order to enhance the region and to provide a federal counterweight to the PQ in Quebec. His believers have used taxpayer monies to assist special interest groups in their attempts to make Ottawa officially bilingual and to successfully keep the Montfort hospital open despite the Provincial plans to restructure health services in the area. Constitutionally Ontario is responsible for providing health services yet the federal liberals take every opportunity, at any expense, to protect and project their failed bilingual policy. Anyone who is involved with the system knows that the Ottawa General Hospital is bilingual and provides services in both official languages; therefore the Montfort is not needed for that reason. It is needed however for the hordes of Quebecers who come to Ontario for treatment. And yes, Ontario doctors and hospitals do not receive full compensation as rates for Quebec are less than for Ontario. Again, Ontarians lose and Quebecers win while governments look the other way. Similarly, the federal government has interfered with the Ontario government and funded private groups in an attempt to make Ottawa officially bilingual.

Trudeau, the world traveller long before he came to government, was familiar with the problems of the third world. He ensured that Canada dispensed billions to countries in foreign aid so that we would be perceived as open and generous worldwide. But those grants and aid cost those countries dearly since they were compelled to buy from us or use our services in return. The return to Canada was usually in the realm of 125%. This was not, and is not, the way to foster economic development and freedom offshore. "Instead of making grants to foreign governments in the name of economic aid — and thereby promoting socialism — while at the same time imposing restrictions on the products they succeed in producing- and thereby hindering free enterprise-we could assume a consistent and principled stance."[1] Trudeau was not a free trader and opposed any such notion. Similarly, the current liberal government, who campaigned on the promise of reversing free trade with the U.S. and Mexico, have not done so. This has been good for Canadian consumers despite the naysayers such as Maude Barlow and her Council of Canadians, also funded in part by taxpayer's money. One can only hope the liberal conversion to free trade and more free markets lasts.

A quick scan through David Somerville's book, *"Trudeau Revealed: Through his Actions and Words"*, will reveal a host of names thrust to prominence when Trudeau became Prime Minister through their association with him in his youth, schooling, travels, and early political writing and activism. Of note is the absence of English Canadians. Many of these people benefited through Prime Minister Appointments. There is much doubt that they would have achieved their positions other than by their association or friendship with Trudeau.

If you follow the rules and don't ask questions you will be rewarded assuming you can be ruthless and heartless simultaneously. This is an important characteristic in both crime and politics.

End Notes

1. Milton Friedman, "*Capitalism and Freedom, 4th Ed.*," Chicago: University of Chicago Press, 2002, p. 74.

20

Exclusive

Few people had the ear of Trudeau, he kept his own counsel. His trusted allies from Quebec, Lalonde, Pelletier, and Marchand were at his side initially but soon moved on to less exhaustive posts or appointments. They were not replaced. It is often stated that Trudeau emulated Louis XIV who was quoted as stating: "L'etat c'est moi". Certainly at times Trudeau appeared bigger than life but it was a calculated presence. He did not have a large number of confidants because he had no equals, at least in his own mind. More importantly, it is not possible to shepherd plots and plans when the knowledge is shared by too many. In reality he governed alone, as a monarch or more accurately a seignior. Trudeau considered the French his flock and he was determined to give them the rewards that their English masters had supposedly withheld over the decades since the defeat of the French on the Plains of Abraham. This was "social justice" in his mind and therefore in order to maintain secrecy and keep the deception effective, he kept to himself. Insofar as the conspiracy that brought Trudeau to Ottawa there were no new members and those that were aware kept the secret and still do.

21

Fortitude

There is no doubt that Trudeau showed great fortitude. Just the mere fact alone that he was prepared to and did challenge the State and sought to make it over into his image or vision is proof enough. To the end he fought to maintain his influence over the future of Canada. His open letters on the subject of Meech Lake and the Charlottetown accords reinforced his belief in the legislative and social reforms he had championed. No intelligent person would challenge his commitment to his goals; however, there are lots to challenge insofar as those goals are destructive rather than constructive to Canada internally and internationally. Any reasonable person will acknowledge that although he campaigned repeatedly on unity he brought this country closer to disunity than any other PM with the possible exception of Mackenzie King. Furthermore, Canada commanded more respect and influence internationally when he came to power than when he left.

In a determined effort to force his "third option" he forced the country to convert to the metric system so that it would conform to the European standard. This was remarkably ill advised since 80% of our trade is with the U.S. which continues to use the imperial system. To this day the system has not really taken and even young Canadians are disinclined to use metric. This was a very expensive transition that did not in any way affect the European response to our trading overtures. More importantly, it was not something that the people of Canada wanted but PET did. So much for representative government!

His abhorrence of nuclear weapons and anything military led him to destroy the fighting capability of the Canadian Forces, among other reasons. Not patriotic in a military sense, he was not inclined to serve his country during the Second or Korean Wars. He was either travelling or studying abroad. This aside, I am sure that he reflected on his ethnic origins on matters military. There is no doubt, based on his emasculating of Canada's legitimately proud services that he was following some of Napoleon's maxims. Specifically, "The first quality of a soldier is constancy in enduring fatigue and hardship. Courage is only the second. Poverty, privation and want are the school of the good soldier."[1] With successive budget cuts and lack of sufficient pay many of our military have had to resort to welfare under Trudeau's and successive governments. Also, with the selection of his Chief of Defence Staffs and those selected by successive governments we see that he chose not to select men of character who would follow this Napoleonic maxim: "A general-in-chief cannot exonerate himself from responsibility for his faults by pleading an order of his sovereign or the minister ... Hence it follows that every general-in-chief who undertakes to execute a plan which he knows to be bad, is culpable. He should communicate his reasons, insist on a change of plan and finally resign his commission rather than become the instrument of his army's ruin."[2] You have seen an example of this where a Canadian Commander of a UN mission probably should have resigned when the UN failed to support his plan. Had he done so more attention would have been drawn to the situation and many lives may have been spared. Almost to a man in the last 40 some years the individuals selected to head the armed forces, handpicked by the Prime Minister, have been selected because they were committed to whatever political end the Prime Minister and the Defence Minister wanted. As such they have all overseen the insipient ruin of the Canadian Armed Forces. It is a national shame!

End Notes

1. Phillips, "*Roots of Strategy*," Mechanicsburg: Stackpole Books, 1985, p. 425.
2. Ibid., p. 429.

22

Fatalistic

Nothing brings the multitudes to seek the aid of government than the hint of an epidemic or some future bug for which there may be a cure. Trudeau's hit man on Alberta oil, the honourable Marc was later Minister of Health, and he saw such an opportunity when the rumour of swine flu was captured and amplified to an "apprehended medical insurrection". Anxious to protect the public from a pervasive and killer virus the federal government lavished millions on Connaught laboratories in Hull, Quebec in order to produce enough vaccine to float the Titanic. In addition, they spent monies on advertising in order to whip the public into a fearful frenzy. I remember this episode of hype well because I refused to accept the shot even though I was ordered to take it. It was subsequently dispensed to the old and the necessary, some of whom died from the shot rather than the flu. Fortunately, as in many other instances, the government was wrong and we were spared the scourge but not the expense. The trick is to predict the worst and if it doesn't turn out that bad then you can claim credit for your action or inaction. We have seen this repeatedly in recent years where the federal government predicts either large deficits or small surpluses and when it turns out that the deficits were smaller or the surpluses larger then it was because of good management by the government. False claims and exaggerated claims are all part of the spin and the media and public never seem to catch on. However, from a political perspective it is better to be pessimistic and be wrong than optimistic.

Paranoia is good in both crime and politics.

23

Honour

It is always interesting to listen to the way politicians use or confuse the word "Honour". There are certain elements to the word that politicians rarely respect, at least in Canada. Truth which was commented on earlier is one of them. Politicians are great manipulators of facts and Trudeau was as well. Honour also embeds the concept of doing what is right and a sense of duty to the citizens of the country. Trudeau and his governments were often wrong, and occasionally admitted it long after the fact, but their sense of duty was skewed towards Quebec to the annoyance and exclusion of other parts of Canada. If you read Trudeau's views about Canadian natives, for example, you would expect that he would have done something significant to improve their lot. He did not. Oh yes, he did throw lots of taxpayer money their way but the natives were more or less left to their own design. Years later we find the situation for Canadian natives worse than ever despite the monies wasted. The current PM was once the Minister of Indian and Northern Affairs in the Trudeau government and he has done precious little as well. The treatment of our natives is a national shame and we can hardly claim that our treatment of them is honourable. To get a different view, a native view, I would recommend the chapter on the "Iroquois" in *"Stolen Continents"* by Ronald Wright. No wonder they dishonour us publicly both domestically and internationally. Yet we go all over the world preaching to others about human rights. As a final point on honour, I would encourage each citizen to watch the Question Period on television just once. You might as well you are paying for it. You will be able to determine for yourselves that there is little honour in the conduct of your representatives. Most of them can't even ask a question without referring to notes or reading it verbatim. This is forbidden according to the House rules but is overlooked because of the poor quality of individual elected. This applies to all parties and in both official languages.

Although not directly responsible Trudeau set the low standard for honourable action by governments and it was liberal governments that have acted with dishonour in relations with our veterans, the very people who put their lives at risk for the country. We know that Trudeau was a pacifist and anti-military and that his policies have prevailed within the federal governments since he ruled. But it brings dishonour on government and the citizens of this country when we find that the government has mismanaged the pensions of its veterans and refuses to give the veterans their due. The liberals have challenged the legitimate claims of the veterans in court in an effort to avoid accountability. Similarly, they were responsible for imposing a lesser entitlement on native veterans and initially resorted to the courts in order to thwart the legitimate claims of these citizens. Finally, how honourable is our very own Prime Minister who has resorted to several legal challenges to his own ethics counsellor over his financial and ministerial activities while in office?

Yes, there is honour among thieves and both the Mafia and politicians qualify.

24

Ideals

Someone once said that "an idea is not responsible for who believes in it." How true! One wonders then why supposedly intelligent reasonably affluent people believe in socialism. If you research the subject you will find that many of the socialist proponents hail from privileged status yet for some reason believe that revolution will lead to socialist nirvana. Revolutionaries like Castro and Che Chevara and countless others have overthrown brutal regimes only to replace them with corrupt and incompetent ones. It is hard to see why anyone would laud and celebrate socialist countries such as Russia or Cuba or China where the evidence is substantial that socialism only works for the elite. The problems are numerous and monumental such as corruption, central planning failures of every variety, lack of security, lack of food, primeval medical capability, black markets, police brutality, alcoholism, food lines (when food is available), lack of consumer goods, environmental pollution, lawlessness, etc. No wonder some of them are moving to democratic countries with market economies. What was it that attracted PET to move on China before Nixon, celebrate and encourage Castro, treat Mao as if he were superhuman? Perhaps it was PETs rabid anti-Americanism or just that he believed that socialism was the answer to the world's problems. In any event history has yet to write the final chapter on socialism (China) but it is inevitable that China will fail as a collective society. It is also true that all of PETs attempts to advance socialist regimes and socialism in general served to alienate the U.S. towards Canada and came to nothing except to lengthen his FBI file. As a footnote it may be that his apprenticeship under Pearson (a known socialist supporter) made him lean too far left. Whatever the case he was responsible for some of the monumental social programs that resulted in Canada's current egregious debt situation. The propensity for the liberals to strike monopolies such as Medicare, only to find them inefficient, ineffective, and wholly uneconomical lingers. The government is simply too involved with goods other than public goods. Private industry can and will deliver them more effectively, efficiently and economically than any government. Regrettably, in Canada we carried on so that now we are saddled with marketing boards, Medicare, equalization, excessive taxation, and a federal government far too involved in everyday Canadian life. We need to remind ourselves, from time to time, that although ideals are rarely if ever achieved, they are almost always worth striving for. Capitalism and Democracy have and will help us achieve a better society than socialism ever will.

25

Elite

In addition to being a dandy, PET was an elitist. The term narcissist fitted him perfectly. When I was younger and I heard the Carly Simon song, "*You're So Vain*", I always thought of Trudeau. In his book, Michael Bliss referred to him, in a subtitle to a picture, as "*an elite of one*". Trudeau was openly proud of his supposed intellectual superiority and upper class snobbery. Again, many mistook arrogance for intelligence. He went to extremes to belittle others and insult those he considered inferior. His pirouette behind the Queen, his finger to citizens at Salmon Arm and his infamous "fuddle duddle" demonstrated his contempt for the monarchy, the working class, parliament, and his critics. His drive for the National Arts Centre a national gallery and unstinting support for the Arts reflected his snobbery and contempt for the working man whose taxes were lavished on Canadian artists. He abolished the traditional system of honours and awards and created a uniquely Canadian system. He destroyed the traditions of the Canadian military and substituted social engineering in order to advance francophones through the B&B program.

His new system of awards and honours was biased to the Canadian elite. Writers, painters, media, entertainers, academics, and the political elite have been the benefactors. The working man and woman have been largely ignored and remain so today. It is a sad commentary that the people who have built and support this country are rarely honoured. Regrettably, the recipients of this political largess have contributed little to the country other than to support the socialists and their political masters. It was and is the little guy who works in the fields, factories, small businesses, primary industries, mines, forests, and other salaried employees who are responsible for generating Canada's wealth. Regrettably they rarely receive credit. It goes to those appointed by politicians or funded by governments or supporting governments who get the goodies.

Trudeau was not shy in his condescending and paternalistic approach to the public. He did not think their thoughts or ideas merited much attention. Again, Professor Hayek comments on this type of approach and why it happens: "Probably it is true enough that the great majority are rarely capable of thinking independently, that on most questions they accept views which they find ready-made, and that they will be equally content if born or coaxed into one set of beliefs or another."[1] The trick then is to make them belief what you want them to believe. This is where truth challenges spin and spin wins.

The power to reward and provide grants and tax monies to our so called artists has been a powerful intoxicant for their thirst for political favour. In short they have sold their souls and been indoctrinated into believing the "lie" that is socialism. The latest sham is the appointment of the Canadian answer to Barbara Walters, lady Pamella, (Wallen) to a foreign post merely reinforces the lust for largesse of this group and further ingratiates and enslaves them to the socialist cause. Another example of this sop to achievement is the list of recipients of the Order of Canada. If you look closely you will find that it is much like Cabinet building in that it is constructed based on race, religion, region, sex, and heavily weighted in favour of politicians, entertainers, media personalities, artists (many of whom are unknown outside Canada and depend on grants from government to live; those who really have talent go elsewhere) and the other members of the Canadian elite. This process of political appointments, perfected and exploited by Trudeau, has become a national shame and has tanked morale in the Foreign Service. The current PM continues this orgy of largess by the appointment of Alphonso to the court of Denmark.

There are some things I can agree with in the Maude Barlow and Bruce Campbell book entitled *"Straight through the Heart"*, their answer to Chrétien's *"Straight From the Heart"*. "Fundamental change is possible, but only when elites are faced with a very real threat to their system of wealth and privilege."[2] I can also agree with some of their recommendations such as, become politically literate, become politically active, become economically literate, and grow leaders from the grass roots. The political elite and political parties have a stranglehold on politics in Canada and this must be changed.

End Notes

1. Hayek, *"The Road to Serfdom,"* Chicago: University of Chicago Press, 1994, p. 180.
2. Barlow and Campbell, *"Straight Through the Heart,"* Toronto: HarperCollins, 1996, p. 273.

26

The Sun King

No PM before or since Trudeau has consolidated power unto himself in such a glutinous and heavy handed way. His creation of the PMO brought his advisors to the forefront of the political hierarchy second only to him. It even relegated Cabinet Ministers to secondary status and shoved mere mortals (MPs) down another rung on the food chain. Yet he demanded blind trust and loyalty. This was not difficult because he used his considerable charisma to woo not only liberals but the elites of the country. To secure votes and seats in other regions he used the traditional tool of patronage and largess. For Quebecers he nurtured the perception that only he represented the true aspirations for Quebec within Canada and he swept Quebec in each of his governments.

Trudeau was a smart ass and a bully. He changed the way we do business and government in this country from one of guarded co-operation to confrontation and open conflict. It remains so today. As Kimon Valaskakis points out in his book, *"Canada in the Nineties – Meltdown or Renaissance?"*, Canadian internal activities are marked by several kinds of confrontation. Here is a short list of examples: First, we have the never ending confrontations between the federal and provincial governments often leaving the cleanup to the municipalities and city governments. Next, we have the competition and conflict between public and private industries. We have governments providing medical care, insurance, banking, air transportation, rail transportation, policing, utilities, pensions, alcohol distribution, communications, postal service, publishing and a host of other goods and services in direct competition with private industry that could provide it more economically, effectively, and efficiently. The number of Crown corporations and agencies providing services goes far beyond need. This denies the economies of scale to industries that could permit them to compete globally. Also, we have the dysfunctional labour/management conflict that permeates our industries and government led by the totally inept collect bargaining model introduced by Trudeau. This is a model of how not to do things in which everyone loses especially the citizens of Canada. Trudeau lead us down this path but we must find a way of working better together or Canada will remain a backwater in the global scheme. Our penchant for treating our fellow Canadians worse than our neighbours or trading partners is a recipe for continued discord and lost potential.

Trudeau had no use for Parliament regardless of which side of the House an MP inhabited. In an essay he wrote entitled, *"Some Obstacles to Democracy in Quebec"*, he expressed his view of liberal MPs: "The shameful incompetence of the average Liberal M.P. from Quebec was a welcome asset to a Government that needed little more than a herd of performing asses to file in when the division bell rang. The party strategists had but to find an acceptable stablemaster... and the trained donkeys sitting in the back benches could be trusted to behave."[1] After serving as Prime Minister a few years he had this to say about the opposition: "When they (the Opposition) get home, when they get out of Parliament, when they are 50 yards from Parliament Hill, they are no longer Honourable Members — they are just nobodies." "I think we should encourage the Opposition to leave. Every time they do, the I.Q. of the House rises considerably."[2] The liberal party of today demonstrates the same lack of respect for their own MPs and the Opposition, every day. As a consequence, they have continued the deterioration of Parliament to an ineffectual institution. It cannot be good, for any country, when its primary institution and symbol of democracy is held up to such ridicule and scorn. Why then would good honest people of character want to be part of such a body?

In addition to establishing the PMO he created an inner cabinet committee, filled with his Quebec lieutenants, that was entitled Plans and Priority, which he chaired. It was the senior cabinet committee and oversaw all of the government activities. Along with this came review and alteration of the various cabinet committees that lead to his Quebec allies consolidating power within the Cabinet and the government. By appointing francophone ministers to the key government departments he ensured that his plans to take over the bureaucracy using the tool of B&B could not be thwarted. In this manner he was sure that using the system of rewards within the public service he could effectively control the federal bureaucracy by promoting to the top jobs. He succeeded beyond his own expectations and effectively politicized the federal public service that had previously enjoyed an enviable international reputation for independence and skill. From Trudeau's reign to the present the federal bureaucracy has continued to deteriorate in effectiveness and efficiency. While publicly defending the principle of merit in the promotion system Trudeau oversaw the destruction of this principle of administration within the public service.

There was no doubt that he was the boss as he posed

often in his gunslinger stance. He took on all comers but especially liked to overpower Provincial Premiers as in the Lougheed case with the NEP. He took every opportunity to consolidate power at the federal level at the expense of provincial and municipal governments who had to come hat in hand to Ottawa for money and support for their programs. He even managed to oversee and then include the equalization process in the constitution, thus taking credit for the generosity of the have Provinces towards the have-nots. Under the formula Quebec was ensured the lions share and this remains so today. This institutionalized provincial welfare has been in effect for approximately 40 years now and none of the have-nots have moved up. Occasionally BC and Ontario have moved down, thanks to NDP governments even more socialistic than the liberals, but Ontario refused to take the money due to provincial pride. This failed policy, instituted under the guise of social justice serves to keep the have-nots in a dependent state which is good only if you look at it from the federal perspective. It represents another example of Trudeau consolidating power and ensuring that the feds retain control and primacy in the hierarchy.

It should be noted here that Alberta and Ontario achieved surpluses in their budgeting and effectively embarrassed the liberal federal government to do the same otherwise our debt could be much worse than it is, if that's possible. Second, these were fiscally responsible governments. In short, the "haves" have taken effective action fiscally whereas the "have-nots" have not. The equalization formula comes up for review in 2004 and despite the guarantee put in the constitution by Trudeau the Premiers of the "have" provinces should insist on changes. This program has stifled initiative and rewarded failures to the tune of $billions in failed ventures (remember the cucumbers in PEI and Newfoundland) and lost opportunities to put the monies into investments that give a return. The liberals have and will continue to spend good money on bad ideas unless they are stopped. The generous people of Ontario and Alberta deserve better and should not be asked to accept a lower standard of living simply so others can continue to receive hand outs. Equalization is not a success story in any sense but it gives the liberals power and rewards their friends and buys votes.

End Notes

1. David Somerville, "*Trudeau Revealed: By His Actions and Words,*" Richmond Hill, BMG Publishing Ltd., 1978, p. 123.
2. Ibid., p. 205.

27

The Socialists Within

The liberal party of the 90's was beset with an internal struggle between the socialists and the fiscal conservatives. Lloyd Axworthy, or Lord Axworthy as he was tagged, the champion of the left, eventually left the government when it was clear that his views were being rejected and those of Paul Martin were being accepted. But during Trudeau's governments there was no shortage of special interests to push the government towards financial ruin under the banner of Social Justice. In *"Straight through the Heart"*, Barlow and Campbell make the point. "It is under Liberal governments that feminists, environmentalists, farmers, aboriginal peoples, peace activists, and a variety of other social advocates have been funded."[1] Thankfully, this process has been reversed by the very same liberals much to the chagrin of these authors. Their book is a scathing attack on any government that does not push the social agenda, despite the costs. They seem to reject the concept that someone will eventually have to pay. Like the NDP they must dream each night of the "Guaranteed Annual Income" a socialist proposal that has sought but not yet found funding. They reject the reversal of social spending in the 90's as necessary to counter our debt ridden financial situation and accuse the government of the day of expedience. Although PET set the stage for this potential Canadian bankruptcy, even he did not condemn his disciple Chrétien for rolling back the social juggernaught in order to preserve our solvency.

In *"The Trouble with Canada"* W. Gairdner gives us an analogy of the different styles of governance that anyone can understand. It is simple but revealing and demonstrates where Canada has been and where it is going under liberal and other political parties. He uses the farmer with two cows' comparison. Under communism, the government confiscates both cows, and sells him back some of the milk. Remember NEP where Ottawa set itself up in the oil industry and confiscated much of the revenue as well as a cut in the future oil fields. Under socialism, the government takes one of the cows and gives it to his neighbour. Equalization is the current example and it has been in effect for 40 years yet none of the have-nots has emerged from their receiver status. Under democratic capitalism, he gets to sell one of the cows, and buys a bull. This is where you are permitted to use your resources and initiative to rise or fall based on risks taken and rewards available.

It is not hard to establish, if you reflect for just a few moments, that socialism is alive and well and flourishing in Canada. Democracy and capitalism are on the wane. Let us hope that we do not elect another Trudeau or Trudeau clone that will complete the journey to totalitarianism. It could happen and those who think otherwise are on another planet. We are infested with socialists and they influence the government every day in every way. There are lobbyists and special interest groups and countless causes that want the government to fund their issue. But Canadians don't have a say as to whether this or that, will be successful. The majority or minority party forming the government, with assist from the NDP, can carry the vote and we become locked into another program that benefits the few at the expense of many. Worse still, it is not just the federal government. Just look at what the NDP did in four years in Ontario. Ontarians went from a have status to a have not one almost overnight. Yet Rae himself, wisely rejected in the next election, continues to receive gratuitous assignments from the grateful federal liberals as he was instrumental in passing bilingual legislation in Ontario. He was always prepared to back the liberal or Tory government in Ottawa when they brought forth another social program. He was rejected after four years by both left and right but for obviously different reasons. For socialists he had failed them. James Laxer points out in his book, "*In Search of a New Left*", why there will always be a strong left movement in Canada. "What causes the party of equality to spring back from the very edge of extinction, however, is the reality of the human condition. It is wealth, privilege and the power of a few to decide the fate of the many that gives rise to a new left when an old one falls by the wayside."[2] Unfortunately, for Canadians it is the socialists in Canada who represent the wealth, privilege, and power. Hence, no uprising need happen unless it comes from the poor, the unprivileged, and the powerless. There will always be those who wish to restrict freedoms and impose taxes on some for the special interests of others. The liberal party has become expert at this but for socialists even they fail to go far enough.

Socialists simply cannot accept that government is not there to solve every social problem. It is there to ensure that problems can be solved through peaceful means without the threat of violence or coercion. It does this by providing for basic public needs such as security, sustenance, medical care, housing assistance, education, justice, law and order. When it goes beyond public needs it is now in the realm of public "wants". Socialists reject out of hand any idea of a needs test for social assistance.

However, in everyday life Canadians face this issue every day. There are any number of things that people want but there are few that they really need. If you want to proceed beyond the basics already provided, the government has created an environment that will allow you to succeed without providing directly. However, it expects you to use your initiative and ingenuity to proceed. Those who are unwilling to put in the effort or personal sacrifice should not expect the government to come to their aid. Similarly, if you take risks, as many businesses and people do, you should not expect the government to bail you out if you fail. The other truth that socialists reject is that private industry can normally provide goods and services more effectively, efficiently and economically than government through competition. "Whatever activity government engages in tends to cost roughly twice as much as the same activity carried out by private entities."[3] Governments simply don't compete and they have no bottom line; there is just that limitless benevolent called the taxpayer who currently works half the year to provide the governments with finances to do what we already require of them. It is enough! Even the current band of socialists in Ottawa has figured it out; Trudeau never did.

Unfortunately, in Canada there is little appreciation for how fortunate we are. Why do so many people want to immigrate here? If you travel the world a bit it becomes immediately obvious. Our government has created the right kind of environment for some people to succeed. And, it aids those who have fallen on misfortune or are unable to assist themselves. However, there is a limit and that socialists fail to recognize. Our tax burden is now driving our trained and talented people away. Similarly, businesses are moving their headquarters to other countries where the tax burden is less onerous. Highly skilled workers are leaving Canada in order to get a better return on their efforts and to escape the heavy handed government interference in their workplace and families. Despite the evidence that confirms we have gone beyond the acceptable taxation limits the socialists among us continue to push governments to do more.

End Notes

1. Barlow and Campbell, *"Straight Through the Heart,"* Toronto: HarperCollins, 1996, p. 9.
2. James Laxer, *"In Search of a New Left,"* Toronto: Penguin Books, 1997, pp. 222–223.
3. Scott Reid, *"Lament For a Notion,"* Vancouver: Arsenal Pulp Press, 1993, p. 254.

28

Economics

Educated initially at university as an economist one is amazed at how poorly Trudeau managed the economy while in power. A confirmed Keynesian he attempted through good times and bad to manage it through government intervention and government spending. He came to power with virtually no federal debt and according to Edward Greenspon and Anthony Wilson-Smith writing in *"Double Vision"* he left office with $199 billion in debt, up from $27 billion in 1974-75. They also point out that Trudeau warned in 1972 that: "If a government wants to do the popular things, it will ruin the economy — real quick". He then proceeded to do just that. In his final year in office, 1984-85, his government spent $100 billion with a deficit of $38.6 billion. Deficit spending financed his social programs and led to a decline in the value of the dollar (it became ridiculed as Trudough), a decline in our international debt rating, an increase in inflation, an increase in unemployment, lack of growth, instability in prices, wage and price controls, six & five increases in salaries to follow, interest rates never before seen in Canada except for the chartered banks and the Mafia, and a central bank fixated on controlling inflation. His governments and those subsequent forced a contraction in the economy and a rollback of federal spending to convince the international financial markets that Canada was still a viable country. We came precipitously close to hitting the wall, as some other countries did, thankfully we did not have to suffer the dictates of the International Monetary Fund and World Bank but we are still servicing this mountain of debt which amounts to negative investment. And we are not out of the woods yet.

For the better part of 15 years, while Trudeau and Levesque were locked in their dance of death over the hearts of Quebecers, the country was being visited by some of the negative consequences of their actions. Nothing spurs investment like political instability and not only did capital flight from Canada but it became increasingly harder to attract capital investment to Canada and particularly Quebec. People and businesses fled Quebec; Montreal once a cosmopolitan city took on the image of a ghost town as businesses and the English left town. When Bill 101 became law this situation accelerated. The age old rivalry between Montreal and Toronto, that kept both vital, became victim to the PQ government that spurned Montreal and embraced Quebec City. International markets and financiers found places other than Canada to invest and there are lots of those.

The first and most visible was the exodus of Sun Life Insurance. Not only did they leave but they were not reticent about telling people why. In this one industry the departures were compelling. "In 1960, over 160 insurance companies were doing business other than sales in Montreal, ... Yet, by the time Sun Life made their announcement, the number of companies had dwindled to fewer than thirty, most of the decline having occurred before the P.Q. victory but during the ultra-nationalist thrust of the 60s and early 70s."[1] It is significant to note that it was the political uncertainty that sparked the exodus fanned by the disunity musings of Trudeau that generated the decline. It is impossible to estimate the cost to Canada economically of this manufactured duel but it helped to erode our standard of living and our international influence over the entire period of Trudeau's stewardship. He must have been aware of the negative consequences of his actions but for him once the battle was joined there would be no turning back despite the negative consequences. The deleterious effects of his quest for unity remain today and have created more generations of Quebecers who will remember another chapter of what they consider to be Canadian betrayal. Ironically, while Trudeau tried to sew unity he and we reaped the economic drought consistent with internal dissent and discord. Overall, his vision of a united country under a repatriated constitution with unanimous support of all provinces complete with a Charter of Rights and Freedoms and an agreed amending formula failed; not only politically but with an enormous price tag. Looking back it is hard to imagine that it was all worth it. Would we not have been better off if this vision had never emerged? It is a tarnished legacy to an unfulfilled ego.

By Trudeau's own admission he and his minions failed badly but what was worse for the economy was his view of the solution: "We haven't been able to make it work, the free market system... the government is going to have to take a larger role in running institutions... It means there is going to be not less authority in our lives but perhaps more..."[2]

And they did get more involved. "The second Trudeau government took the limits off public spending. Egged on by the NDP, it raised welfare payments of all kinds, indexing many of them to the cost of living. It used direct controls to limit domestic petroleum prices, levied huge taxes on petroleum exports, and spent that windfall to subsidize imports."³ Schemes were set up to arrest unemployment and monies were funnelled into industries. Movement grants were established to move the workers to the work but there was a snag. It turned out the people would rather stay in depressed areas and subsist on welfare and the very generous 10/42 unemployment program at the time (work ten weeks and draw UI for 42). Regrettably, the regional development programs continue today with similar results — more good money chasing bad, a concept or theory taught in Economics 101. Bliss sums it up best: "The answers to most Canadian problems – the decade-long search for a credible industrial policy, for example — seemed to boil down to more grants, more studies, more civil servants."⁴ Bliss describes the economic planning of the Trudeau government in the 80s:

> Industrial bailouts kept marginal companies alive at heavy costs to the taxpayer, and caused every failing firm in the country to whine for government help. Regional "equalization" had bound most of Atlantic Canada and large parts of Quebec in whining dependence on a constant flow of federal cheques. The attempt to control foreign investment (Foreign Investment Review Agency) had deterred it, hurting the Canadian economy. Everywhere they had been applied, the visible hands of the planning generation had been clumsy, unproductive, damaging. In 1983 Trudeau's ageing wizards unveiled a special Scientific Research Tax Credit, designed to stimulate research and development on industrial frontiers. In 1984 they suspended it in the face of $2.8 billion in losses to the federal treasury and mounting evidence of complete chaos in its administration."⁵

Strangely, Trudeau delivered funds to Quebec in the same manner as he had criticized other PM's for doing during the Duplessis era. Bowering describes the manner in which Duplessis manipulated Ottawa and Quebec citizens: "He never stopped demanding money from Ottawa, and when it arrived he moved it into a bag with Quebec's logo on it. Then he reached into it and disbursed some little gifts to the waifs in the street before stashing it where no federal nose could sniff it out."[6] This is the tried and true method of Quebec's relationship with Ottawa; it was not invented by the PQ or the BQ. The Quebec government dispenses monies from Canadian taxpayers, cries that it is not enough, insults us at the same time and while so engaged enflames Quebecers with spin about how the rest of Canada has abused them.

By this time, the twilight of the liberal run, the deficits were alarmingly high. In three years between 1979 and 1983 they ran up a total deficit of $68 billion. In 1984 their deficit was a cool $38.6 billion. The accumulation of deficits under Trudeau was passed to the Mulroney government in the form of a crushing national debt. In the initial years of that government they only had a 10% discretionary spending window thanks to the careless and negligent spending habits of the socialists; a situation not unlike today.

Fortunately, through the prudent conservative fiscal planning and later an intelligent liberal and successful businessman fiscal sanity was restored and steps were taken to reverse the trend, following the example of some of the Provinces. He eventually took us to a balanced and then surplus federal budgets but at the expense of our Medicare program. Regrettably, this finance minister has resorted to imaginative accounting and it is not certain what our financial status is at the moment. Unfortunately, only some of the provinces have not followed, most notably Quebec continues to mount serious deficits and debt using the tried and true excuse of blaming Ottawa. One would guess that they expect the rest of Canada to absorb their debts upon independence and no doubt continue equalization payments.

End Notes

1. Albert and Shaw, "*Partition: The Price of Quebec's Independence,*" Point Claire: Thornhill Publishing, 1980, p. 174.
2. David Somerville, "*Trudeau Revealed: By His Actions and Words,*" Richmond Hill: BMG Publishing Ltd., 1978, p. 200.
3. Michael Bliss, "*Right Honourable Men,*" Toronto: HarperCollins Publishers, 1995, p. 260.
4. Ibid., p. 261.
5. Ibid., p. 270.
6. George Bowering, "*Egotists and Autocrats*", Toronto: Penguin Books, 1999, p. 310.

29

Legitimacy

Trudeau never really believed in the Canada he grew up in because he could not shake off the belief that in the beginning the French were set upon and deprived. Even today Quebecers take pride in remembering their defeat as evidenced on their license plates "je m' souvien". The French and then the Quebecers have always felt like second citizens and have never had the courage to step up to the plate and act like equals or take the lead as Canadiens. They have chosen to take the cowardly route and blame the rest of Canada for their malaise and backwardness. This worked well for the clergy and later for politicians until Mr. Lesage sought to break them out of the paradigm. Unfortunately, the French did not rise to the challenge and soon thereafter Mr. Bourassa, a descendant of another complainer, took over the premiership and plunged Quebec and Quebecers back into their inferiority complex.

Trudeau, very aware of the history, decided that he alone could restore French primacy by taking over control of the federal government and thereby win for the French the battle for Canada. To a certain degree he has succeeded but in so doing he has taken an emerging giant back to being a diminished star. Trudeau, with the frustration of decades decided on a zero-sum game in which the French would win at the expense of the rest of Canada. Hence, if you look at his political efforts you will see that they all were created in order to elevate Quebecers and seize control of the levers of power while relegating "Les Anglais" to a supporting role. Quebec has since 1933 known how to control the federal government through careful voting. Aware of the political currents prior to each election they have voted massively to support the leading party in the then more or less two party system. By doing so they gained cabinet posts whereby they could influence government policy. This worked with the exception of the Diefenbaker government of 1957.

Essentially this voting solidarity carried Quebec to power federally until Trudeau arrived on the scene and effectively broke the Liberal/Conservative nature of Canadian politics. Of course there had been third parties before but they were never very prominent. The rise of the PQ within Quebec politics and the BQ federally represent the antithesis to Trudeau's vision of Quebec within Canada. These parties wish to achieve their goals by reasserting the tried and true method of achieving appeasement by deftly employing the threat of succession notwithstanding that that threat doesn't hold with the majority of Canadians anymore. That gambit has been exposed as a great leap backward, even by Quebecers themselves as evidenced by the studies commissioned by the Quebec government prior to the last referendum on independence that remain secret because they do not support separation. In short, the PQ does not have the character to tell Quebecers the truth.

With the arrival of Trudeau and his disciples a sea change was inevitable. He was prepared to effectively seize control of the federal government through the ruthlessness and deception that would have made Machiavelli proud. Cloaking his plans and programs in subterfuge he would attempt and succeed at putting Quebecers in power through his power. He did this through the alteration of the B&B commission recommendations, the use of reverse discrimination, the slow but progressive erosion of the English traditions, the alienation of the West, the centralization of political power at the federal level, the intrusion into Provincial rights, the appointment of Quebecers to all agencies, courts, and other federal bodies using the B&B 28% apportionment. His plan was to make Quebec a winner after all but unfortunately he neglected to see that this would make Canada a loser in the international game. His plans were the exact opposite to what was needed for Canada to take her rightful place as an emerging power. The tragedy, in part, is that so many Canadians of all ethnic origins believed in him and many still do.

He had charisma and charm but it was a misguided gift because he used it in a negative way. It is akin to voting patterns of recent years where the electorate votes more against a party or leader than for them. His ends may have been supportable but his means were deceptive, wrong, and ultimately have wrought malice, controversy, conflict, and yes racism and hatred in the country. His pro communist stance internationally and socialist government brought nothing but scorn from our main trading partner the US and confusion to our European allies. His attempts to break the ties to the English Monarchy were amateurish and reflected the jealously that inspired them. He was very nearly a very dangerous man. Had he been born in another country he might have been a very destructive force for like others of his kind, the hints were there that this was what he would do. History reveals many zealots and dictators who have revealed their intentions in advance. Often they were discounted until carried out to the detriment of their citizens. Trudeau gave Canada a hint also, in his early writings, but likewise no one seemed to care and most got swept up in the charisma rather than the intent. Much of what he wrote and professed remained obscure outside Quebec yet the intent was there if anyone cared to research it. That his federal liberal opponents in the leadership race chose to ignore it and also the Conservative opposition remains a mystery. Had the research been done it is possible that Trudeaumania could have been defeated and Trudeau exposed for the socialist that he was. Trudeau was not a malevolent dictator but he did employ his characteristics in like manner and did pursue his goals just as fervently.

So what exactly have Trudeau's efforts wrought for Quebec and Canada? It is often quoted that "the whole is greater than the sum of its parts" but that is not true of Trudeau's Canada because all the parts were pulling in different directions. This is manifest in the Charter of Rights and freedoms wherein the governments can do that which citizens cannot. Moreover, Trudeau ensured that the infamous "notwithstanding" clause could be invoked by Quebec. He enshrined equalization into the constitution despite the cumulative evidence that it has a deleterious effect on the "have-nots" and a negative tax effect on the "haves"; everyone loses in another tax rip off that differentiates between Canadians. This was included to ensure that Quebecers would not be penalized for their differences. In effect it was rewarding failure on a Provincial level which is again a negative reward system. His spending on social policies bought Canada a crippling debt that will long outlive the policies. His international policies brought scorn and displeasure from our allies and praise from our protagonists. His economic policies ensured high unemployment, a falling currency, rising debt, debilitating deficits, high interest rates and eventually wage and price controls that confirmed his policies had failed. The bicultural aspects of B&B ensured that thousands would receive promotions and jobs that they did not merit and solidify mediocrity into a once proud and capable public service.

His goal to put Quebecers in charge succeeded while Canada hasn't. He divided and ruled at a time when co-operation and consultation would have been more appropriate. As a consequence, he alienated many regions and treated Canadian extremities as mere supplicants to Central Canada (Ontario & Quebec). Michael Bliss sums up the Trudeau years: "In 1984 the Trudeau Liberals left public finances in a hell of a mess, with the deficit soaring close to $40 billion. It was irresponsibility and incompetence not seen since the days of Laurier's railway policies."[1]

Malcolm Muggeridge, an English reporter summed up Trudeau in the following way: "He's a totally unprincipled man in the ordinary sense of the word. He's seen that in modern government you don't really need to do anything and you don't need to have any views. All you need is a Persona, which is immediately graspable."[2] Hence, we witnessed Trudeaumania the bug that bit millions of Canadians in 1968. I think that Trudeau was the consummate gamesman. The definition of a gamesman, that follows, is one that I used in an essay on the lack of effective leadership in the military. Unfortunately, I cannot locate the source but I include it because it captures much of Trudeau:

> The modern gamesman is best defined as a person who loves change and wants to influence its course. He likes to take calculated risks and is fascinated by technique and new methods. He sees a developing project, human relations, and his own career in terms of options and possibilities, as if they were a game. His character is a collection of near paradoxes understood in terms of its adaptation to the organization requirements. He is co-operative yet competitive; detached and playful but compulsively driven to succeed; a team

player but a would-be superstar; a team leader but often a rebel against bureaucratic hierarchy; fair and unprejudiced but contemptuous of weakness; tough and dominating but not destructive. ...His main goal is to be known as a winner, and his deepest fear is to be labelled a loser.

Trudeau was indeed a man of contradictions but that was a means to keep people at a distance. He was a loner. His marriage ended in divorce after seven years and three sons after which he returned to his life alone. His preffered isolation was assured through his Chiefs of Staff who guarded jealously his exposure even to his cabinet ministers. Nonetheless, he captured Canadians fascination and held it for a time. Time enough for him to work his magic through the illusion of "equality" and "social justice". Time enough for Canada to continue down the road to socialism and eventual oblivion. In the philosophical words of Yogi Berra, we have come to the fork in the road but we took the wrong one.

In his final years in power Trudeau strived, as the elder statesman, to secure peace in the world's hot spots and to generate more aid for the Third world. His sponsorship of the North-South dialogue and world travels were conducted more in the hope of receiving the Nobel Prize for peace than to really help. He did not have much political capital to spend. "He bounced off Margaret Thatcher's solid hair. The Soviet leaders were involved in a parade of funerals. As far as Reagan's USA was concerned, he was just another Beatle."[3] The whole escapade became a farewell tour. The sentiment was right but the sincerity and execution were wanting. "J.L. Granatstein and Robert Bothwell conclude their exhaustive study of Trudeau's foreign policy with the judgement that in foreign affairs he was never a serious thinker, "only an adventurer in ideas with great articulation and little commitment."[4]

In essence, Trudeau took Canada and Canadians on his adventure after which we found ourselves left up the white water creek, in a snowstorm, in his canoe without a paddle to guide us while he took a walk. It would be up to others to get us safely home. Unfortunately, we are still up the creek after 19 years of conservatives and liberals who continue down the socialist fork in the road.

End Notes

1. Michael Bliss, "*Right Honourable Men,*" Toronto: HarperCollins, 1995, p. 274.
2. Richard Gwyn, "*The Northern Magus,*" Toronto: McLelland and Stewart, 1980, p. 322.
3. George Bowering, "*Egotists and Autocrats,*" Toronto: Penguin Books, 1999, p. 448.
4. Michael Bliss, "*Right Honourable Men,*" Toronto: HarperCollins, 1995, pp. 272–273.

30

So What Do We Do Now?

The paradox here is that we, the grassroots, are both the problem and the solution. Let me explain. One of Trudeau's musings is interesting as it relates to the situation we find ourselves in today: "Some legitimate and even convincing cases have been made that in certain countries at certain times that [one-party democracy] is a good form of democracy. I wouldn't be prepared to think I would be successful in arguing that for Canada at the present time, but such times might come, who knows?"[1] Obviously, we have more than one party at the federal level but as long as we keep electing majority governments we are de facto in one-party dictatorships for each 4–5 year span between elections.

This book has used facts and the analysis of many thoughtful individuals to demonstrate that the conspiracy of a few Quebecers is in full bloom and the future of Canada is doubtful. On the day that PET was laid to rest his resurrection was revealed in full view of the Canadian public when his eldest son delivered the eulogy. This was intended, I believe, by the liberal party as the first meaningful exposure of Trudeau's eldest son to begin his ascension to the liberal throne. Like his father before him, he will tour the country seeking exposure and networking after which he will be elected to Parliament in his father's old riding where he will await the call to the leadership. Jean Chrétien will be followed for a short time by an Anglophone (liberal party tradition and Martin will qualify even though he is a Quebecer) and it will then be Justin's time to take over the party and the government. His task will be to continue his father's vision of a Canada ruled by Quebecers. The party made his funeral into a campaign event which reveals the depths to which those people will plunge in order to promote the party. It demonstrates that in politics you live and die by the party.

Canadians can set back and let this revolution continue as they did with PET, by being apathetic and ignoring the election and not vote, or they can retake control of the country and reverse the slide into social ruin. After all, "a state where citizens don't interest themselves in politics is destined to slavery."[2] One of the ways of achieving this as individual voters is to vote once again but with the intent to not elect individuals who are characterized as the guardian moral syndrome purports. It will be necessary for the electorate to select individuals who represent the majority of working Canadians and who hold fast to the Commercial Moral Syndrome. This will not be easy because you will be fighting the established elite with their control of the media and vast financial resources. They will also use every dirty trick in the book and some that aren't there in order to gain and maintain power. Yes, we will have to suffer more spin doctors, such as Warren Kinsella. After all, that is what politics is all about. That said it is incumbent that the right people exercise your power. Failure to do so will result in the same results that have occurred in other socialist states. We do have a choice.

Jeffrey Simpson has suggested some solutions to our electoral dilemma in his book, *"The Friendly Dictatorship"*.

His analysis of voter apathy is thought provoking but there is an additional point that should be made. If we look at voter turnout in the Trudeau years we see that when the liberals were elected we note a rather low voter turnout. Conversely, when they were rejected there was a high voter turnout. This would indicate that the liberal voters are much more loyal and likely to vote than for other parties. Also, we find that since 1993 the voter turnout has been increasingly lower while liberal majorities have been getting bigger. There is a direct correlation then between liberal success and voter turnout. In short, if the other parties want to be successful then they must mobilize the electorate much more than in the recent past. Similarly, voters who do not support the liberals must see that their vote does count and only by exercising it can they exorcise the socialists from political dominance. Simpson goes on to suggest solutions to our political gridlock in Canada and they are all good except for one. His suggestions to reform Parliament, introduce proportional representation, elect the Senate, and change the electoral system all have significant merit. I suppose that his suggestion to increase party strength has some merit if he means that other parties need to strengthen but I would suggest the opposite is more appropriate. We have seen the stranglehold that parties have on their members and the lengths they will go to in order to impose discipline. I would suggest that a looser system with more free votes and a lessening of party discipline would be more beneficial to the system. This would require that parties do a better job of convincing their members that a policy was correct and serendipitously the public would be better informed as well. A current example of the mess we get into with our "friendly dictator" is the Kyoto protocol. The PM has made a decision but no one knows the rationale behind it. As one would expect, all hell has broken out and it is open season on Kyoto. Unfortunately, all the extremists will have their say and the unwashed will remain so. No one will take the logical step of presenting a reasoned and realistic approach. That is what Parliament is for but in its current state nothing of the kind can occur.

Although it is not considered right, for now anyway, to examine someone's character too closely when they present for public office, I think we make a grievous error in not doing so. Once again, referring to the guardian syndrome it is clear that these people are takers not givers. Just try to justify their pension plan! Just try to justify that while everyone else is suffering a decrease in disposable income, they vote themselves a glutinous salary and expense increase and then tie their future salary increases to those (judges) whose salaries they themselves approve. Does this seem to be selfless to you? Do you really want to put people in power of the public purse that cannot see the conflict of interest here?

Appraise them by their deeds not by their words is a maxim for professional investigators and analysts. This is the standard that I have tried to apply to Trudeau and he comes off as an arrogant, deceitful, yet accomplished tyrant. People in Canada have accorded him a high intelligence. True, he was well educated but that doesn't necessarily translate into intelligence. He was arrogant, a characteristic often confused with intelligence. At no point in his memoirs or other writings could it be found that he ever entertained the thought that he might be wrong. Without ever wanting for anything he fits the profile of a revolutionary but only a peaceful one. Not interested in the military, nor particularly patriotic during wartime, he went on to use that same force in order to quell dissent. This dissent was perpetrated under the incompetent police force that he was responsible for. While preaching a program of social justice much of what he achieved was through unjust means. His balanced approach was unbalanced in favour of the French part of his ancestry. Although educated as an economist his economic policies were chaotic and his myopic pursuit of Keynesian policies has put Canada in debt that generations to come will have to contend with. His form of federalism saw only a strong central government that kept the Provinces in check by the use of funds controlled by Ottawa. In his quest for power this tool (tax dollars) was used tactically and strategically to leverage, or counterweight, to use his favourite term, provinces to comply with his vision. He recruited his most powerful ministers from Quebec and elevated thousands of Quebecers to prominent roles within the federal government, courts, arts, and every type of appointment that he controlled. Many of these were unearned or unwarranted and the candidates were not worthy based on their qualifications. If we appraise his policies, plans, and accomplishments appropriately he was less than successful. All he achieved was flawed and built around conflict. He pitted one group against another and squandered taxpayer monies on programs that mostly benefited Quebec.

Trudeau, from the very beginning, used hyphenated-Canadians to set people apart and differentiate. This is a simple but effective form of racism. It accentuates our differences instead of our similarities. So does multiculturalism and biculturalism. If Canada is to remain a country we must remove this scourge of identification. Most everyone here is a Canadian citizen, except for those immigrants who have not yet become citizens. I trace my ancestry through four generations. Surely, that is enough to call myself Canadian and not Irish. Nor do I think of myself as an English-Canadian. As the current phrase goes, I am Canadian and proud of it.

Those who worked for and with him were loyal to a fault. Surely some of them must have been aware of the flaws in the programs and policies that he espoused. Surely some of the senior bureaucrats knew that the bureaucracy was being politicized along with DND and the RCMP. Why did they continue to deny it? Because they were of like minds and were just as likely to be entrapped as to entrap others. The system of rewards and punishment is highly refined and prolific in the public service. It has become so through decades of operation. It will not be eradicated easily, if ever. It does not serve the public well.

But to start we must elect people of character. First, we must discern that they are. We can only do that by exposing their deeds and determining their characteristics through their friends and associates. Surely we have the skill to investigate to the extent to see if they fit the guardian or commercial profile. The next thing that needs to be done is that the media in this country has to do a much better job of gleaning the facts and quit trying to promote themselves. The media should endeavour to present all known sides to any story, not just the ones that support their political beliefs. A free press is only useful if it is objective and thorough. It should not take sides but use principles and logic to present its case. Canadians need to demand to know not just the advantages of a program or policy but the disadvantages as well. They will occur just as surely as the benefits. To do otherwise makes the media a side show of the politicians and mere supplicants of the politically powerful.

We teach our children that any action has consequences, good and bad. They complain later when the disadvantages come calling and are caught unawares; so too with communities and countries. We also teach our children to be self-reliant, pursue education as it is one advantage that generally pays off in reaching your goals. We want our children to be good citizens, those who give and don't take unless absolutely necessary. Unfortunately, in Canada, we are creating a progressively socialist society. We work half a year in order to pay our taxes only to see much of it go to servicing our debt. Sizable amounts go towards social programs that are poorly administered and rife with fraud.

The politicians will tell you that their spending is preferable to other spending but this is economic fraud. These people have progressively replaced the citizen or consumer as the king of the economy. This is wrong. In a democracy it should be the people who decide where their money is spent. We have deferred this role to political parties who choose their leader and govern through coercion, bribery, and deceit. How else could you control 170+ to speak with one voice? Therein lays the paradox. If a leader and his cabinet are prepared to treat members of their own party in this manner why should they worry about the great unwashed? All the politicians need to do is control the propaganda, dispense largess, refuse to trade or compromise, blindly follow their leader, condemn their critics, protect the elite, put on a good show, corrupt the media, refuse to be swayed by facts, appeal to the emotions, and justify actions with honour and they will succeed.

On the other hand, we as thoughtful citizens, who pay the freight, could elect individuals who: respect their fellow citizens, refuse to coerce or bribe, practise as well as preach democracy, respect and deliver on their promises, are honest and forthright, are willing to compete fairly, work easily with others without letting egos get in the way, reach voluntary agreements, rely on competition and initiative to carry the day, actively seek new ways of doing things, are open to change, respect other countries and cultures, dissent only to achieve improvement, are frugal with others money, are positive and hopeful, willingly admit when they have erred, take action rather than reacting, and exercise leadership for the good of all not just some.

We have a choice and it is a clear one but we are failing

badly. The more we ignore the failure of politics and politicians to deal with the difficult problems the worse it gets. This is normal because the more we ignore our institutions the more likely it is that they will be corrupted. Look at what is happening in the world of business today. Shareholders are being fleeced because of the trust they put in company executives while the executives are infected with the greed virus. Likewise with politics! If we continue to let a select group of people, who operate as the guardians do, have uninhibited control of our country for 4–5 years at a time then we will get the same result as shareholders. After all, we are all shareholders in Canada as citizens. If you choose not to exercise your power, as small as it may seem, then you freely relinquish your rights and freedoms to others who may not respect them as you do. In Trudeau, we have seen what happens in a democracy when socialism takes root. Like cancer it spreads until the organism dies. We do not have to take this consequence on blind trust; we have seen it happen in our time to many countries that pursued this route. These same countries are striving to set up democracy and free markets in order to succeed. That should tell us something. It is not too late to turn back and we can do that by exercising our democratic right to vote and select candidates, not parties, whom you know manifest the commercial syndrome.

Canadians are criticized for being apathetic in their politics but that is not totally the case. Young Canadians are disillusioned and disappointed while older ones are far too tolerant. Perhaps we expect too much given the people we elect but to me that is the key. When you observe critically the people in power it is hard not to be discouraged. It seems that the only solution the socialists are capable of is to throw money, our money, at problems. It doesn't work! You have to have a plan; that plan must address root causes; then, you have to make it work and follow up where needed and start over if necessary. Medicare is a case in point. In the mid 90's the feds needed to stem their spending and get their fiscal house in order before the international institutions foreclosed on us. They cut Medicare and then pointed the finger at the provinces. It is true that Medicare needed serious attention but the size of cut was destined to send the system into a spiral. It did. Now we are in the process of studying it to death but it will not be restored until the monopoly is excised and a combination of public and private services are combined to serve Canadians. Moreover, with the aging of the population the emphasis must change in treatment and the cost of drugs. There is much to be done and the current government is hoping the problem will just go away. They have no plan, they have no vision, and they have no business being in charge.

Just as you will now seek to select better candidates for public office it should be made incumbent on the federal government to restore the principle of merit in order to promote or hire the best. Likewise, the large number of appointments now made by the PM should be made independently by a contracted HR organization that would staff the public service in like manner. The company would receive a medium term contract by tender. The military and RCMP would also be required to employ an HR company of professionals to staff their positions and determine promotions under guidelines issued by the respective departments. This would once again ensure equality and equal opportunity. There should be no discrimination or preferential treatment.

Major changes to the policy and plans of the federal government should be subject to referendum approval by the people. We have seen in the recent past that proposals that have cost millions and billions were not wanted by the public. We have also seen that on some questions our representatives were not in agreement with their constituents.

In other cases party discipline required that representatives vote against their constituent's wishes. This needs to stop and can be done through free votes in parliament and referendums, not polls. In short, the public must get more involved in government. Otherwise, we will get poor government because no one else is watching and greed and self-interest will prevail.

As I am writing this we are now in our second year of another socialist government. Since it began, an election that was unnecessary by the way, only one issue has dominated Canadian politics. It is the issue of leadership of the various political parties. First, it was the Canadian Alliance, then the liberals and now the NDP and Conservatives. In other words the politics in Canada revolve around the parties and their problems. But what about Canada's problems you might ask? The reality is that the politicians care less about Canada than about themselves. This is not public service! And if you are looking at role models as politicians take a good look at the CA dissidents. Neither their word nor their signatures were worth anything. They sought to displace a leader duly elected by their untouchable "grass roots". They put themselves above their party, their constituents, and their leader and sought retribution and/or salvation through another party. These are the very types of characters that should never again wield MP power, as little as it is, after the next election. Their constituents should toss them out and select people who more closely represent themselves, hard working commercial syndrome models.

In addition we have seen Joe, totally politically challenged, who holds on to power within the Conservative party to the detriment of both the party and the country. He and his predecessor could have possibly formed part of the government if they had stuck to their principles and joined with their fellow conservatives to present a realistic alternative to the socialists. But no, with sugar plums dancing in his head Joe steadfastly held onto his little corner of the House. This played and still plays right into the hands of the liberals who themselves, after gleefully poking fun at the other parties, are now embroiled in their own internal strife. Why? Because their government is corrupt, inept, irresponsible, and unaccountable and led by the best example of what a politician should not be. The problem with all of this is that Canada is more important than any one or all of them combined. We need to be less tolerant of this type of behaviour and remove these types from power regardless of their political stripe. We need good government regardless of which party provides it but we must guard against those who seek power for powers sake as is the case with the current gang of socialists.

In summary, we followed Trudeau because he was charismatic, a change, and enigmatic at the time. He was fortunate to have leadership qualities but we should have paid more attention to where he planned to lead us. We took a risk since we knew little about him. We should have researched him more. His goal was a socialist state governed by Quebecers. He was partly successful in that we are governed, for the most part, by Quebecers. We are not yet a socialist state but we are on that perilous road. His most grievous legacy is the destruction wrought on the Canadian Parliamentary system and the type of people who seek power through the electoral process at the federal level. They are corrupt and corruptible. Privileged and arrogant they audaciously fumble from issue to issue worried more about spin than truth, visionless beyond the next election, spending from the bottomless treasury, unable to manage anything but waste, irresponsible and unaccountable, prepared to do anything to perpetuate power in the name of their party. We must do better.

Ontario voters are usually responsible for who forms

the government in Ottawa. Unlike Quebecers who follow the tried and true method of block voting for the party that is ahead in the polls or is clearly going to form the government, voters in Ontario do not. Ontario, for example, is clearly responsible for the last two socialist governments. If these voters do not see the wisdom of rejecting this party the next time then we are condemned to more socialist policies and more control by Quebecers. It is time for Ontario to stand up for Canada and not just French-Canada. The liberal MPs of this province have clearly been co-opted by the Quebec federalists to support this region against all else. Unless we want to balkanize this country even more, it is necessary for the people of Ontario to see that they have been deceived and poorly served by their representatives.

It is time for Canadians to take back control of this country. It is time to tell the government and the media that socialism is the wrong solution and that Capitalism and Democracy are the preferred ways to generate growth and freedom. There is no credible argument that demonstrates that the government or any other institution in Canada needs to reflect the population breakdown racially. That in itself is racism and the methods to enforce it require discrimination. Jobs and positions within the federal public service should be open to all but go to the best. Friends, relatives, and subordinates of politicians should not be given preferential treatment with jobs in the public service. Bilingual status in public hiring should be reviewed to reflect real requirements rather than those orchestrated to increase it. It is time to restore reality to a system victimized because of a false premise. Tell your representatives that it is time to stop social engineering; it is morally and ethically wrong-headed.

Canada is a beautiful country filled with thoughtful and generous people. We deserve better but only we can make it so. We are the solution! For the sake of the country get angry! You must assume the mantle of responsibility and admit that apathy, disillusion, and ignorance are not worthy of you or your country. Seek politicians among yourselves who represent you and share your conviction that Canada is the cause and every Canadian has the right to better government. Collectively we must reject socialism and those that seek to impose it. Remember that for every imposition or intervention of government, for every rule and regulation, someone's individual rights have been diminished. We need less government not more. Government is "by" the people in a democracy. We "the people" must come to its aid or suffer the consequences. We need all the people to get active and take their lives into their own hands. It is your future and it is not too late. Do something! Start by getting angry!

Above all, beware the zealous and charismatic! Trudeau has left a legacy that should make Canadians stop and think. He was clearly a gamesman who never hesitated to take us to the brink. He was fiscally irresponsible and came to politics with a clear mission, his attempt to right the perceived wrongs perpetrated on the French by the English, a view that was itself wrong. He used and abused to get his way. He usurped democracy within his party and then within Parliament. By any measure he only partly succeeded. However, he did put in place much that needs to be excised. Canadians need to see the wisdom of restoring honour to our Parliament and public institutions. This can be done by selecting quality candidates who really want to serve Canadians and not themselves and by modifying and updating them. They can also insist on Parliamentary reforms that will return power to the MPs and remove them from the iron grip of political parties. We need men and women of honour who know what it is to succeed in the real world of commerce and bring their successful methods, ideas, knowledge and experiences to do well for the country.

Then we need to support them and work with them and through them to get the kind of legislation we want. We must select people for public office and public service who represent the commercial moral syndrome.
Trudeau challenged Canada. Canada lost!

> *Man will do many things to get himself loved;*
> *he will do all things to get himself envied.*
>
> -Mark Twain

End Notes

1. David Somerville, *"Trudeau Revealed: By His Actions and Words,"* Richmond Hill: BMG Publishing Ltd., p. 199.
2. Ibid., p. 47.

Bibliography

Albert, Lionel, and William F. Shaw. *Partition: The Price of Quebec's Independence*. Point Claire: Thornhill Publishing, 1980.

Andrew. J.V. *Enough!* Kitchner: Andrew Books, 1988.

Barlow, Maude, and Campbel. *Straight Through the Heart*. Toronto: HarperCollins Publishers Ltd., 1996.

Bliss, Michael. *Right Honourable Men*. Toronto: HarperCollins Publishers Ltd., 1995.

Bowering, George. *Egotists and Autocrats*. Toronto: Penguin Books, 1999.

Cameron, Stevie. *On the Take: Crime, Corruption and Greed in the Mulroney Years*. Toronto: MacFarlane Walter & Ross, 1994.

Cossette, Yolanda East. *The Weak Link: Quebec*. Louisville: Imprimerie Gagne Ltee., 1989.

Desbarats, Peter. *Somalia Cover-Up: A Commissioner's Journal*. Toronto: McClelland & Stewart Inc., 1999.

Doern, Russell. *The Battle Over Bilingualism*. Winnipeg: Cambridge Publishers, 1985.

Forster, Victor W. *Let Quebec Go!* Norland: Vic Forster Publishing, 1983.

Friedman, Milton. *Capitalism and Freedom, 4th Ed*. Chicago: The University of Chicago Press, 2002.

Friedman, Milton and Rose. *Tyranny of the Status Quo*. New York: Avon, 1984.

Gairdner, William D. *The Trouble with Canada*. Toronto: General Paperbacks, 1991.

Graham, Ron. *One-Eyed Kings*. Don Mills: Totem Books, 1987.

Greenspon, Edward., and Anthony Wilson-Smith. *Double Vision*. Toronto: Doubleday Canada Ltd., 1996.

Gwyn, Richard. *The Northern Magus*. Toronto: McLelland and Stewart Ltd., 1980.

Hayek, F.A. *The Road to Serfdom*. Chicago: The University of Chicago Press, 1994.

Jacobs, Jane. *Systems of Survival*. Toronto: Random House of Canada Ltd., 1994.

Laxer, James. *In Search of a New Left*. Toronto: Penguin Books, 1997.

Phillips, T.R. Brig.Gen. *Roots of Strategy*. Mechanicsburg: Stackpole Books, 1985.

Rand, Ayn. *Capitalism: The Misunderstood Ideal*. New York: New American Library, 1946.

Reid, Scott. *Canada Remapped*. Vancouver: Arsenal Pulp Press Ltd., 1992.

Reid, Scott. *Lament For a Notion*. Vancouver: Arsenal Pulp Press Ltd., 1993.

Scott, Frank et al. ed. *Quebec States Her Case*. Toronto: Macmillan of Canada, 1964.

Simpson, Jeffrey. *The Friendly Dictatorship*. Toronto: McLelland and Stewart Ltd., 2001.

Somerville, David. *Trudeau Revealed: By His Actions and Words*. Richmond Hill: BMG Publishing Ltd., 1978.

Trudeau, P.E. *The Essential Trudeau*. Toronto: McLelland and Stewart Ltd., 1998.

Trudeau, P.E. *Against the Current*. Toronto: McLelland and Stewart Ltd., 1996.

Trudeau, P.E. and Thomas Axworthy. *Towards a Just Society*. Toronto: McLelland and Stewart Ltd., 1993.

Valaskakis, Kimon. *Canada in the Nineties: Meltdown or Renaissance*. Ottawa: World Media Institute Inc., 1990.

Wright, Ronald. *Stolen Continents*. Toronto: Penguin Books, 1992.

About the Author

Ron Coleman spent 36 years in the RCAF and the CAF, primarily as a pilot on fighters and trainers. He completed an exchange tour with the USAF during the Viet Nam war and later a tour with the United Nations on the Golan Heights.

During his service, he earned a BComm from the Canadian Forces Military College and completed Command and Staff College, and rose to the rank of Colonel before retiring. He has an extensive background in Aviation Safety and spent 10 years as an investigator and manager with the Canadian Transportation Safety Board. He represented Canada in many international accident investigations.

The author is bilingual and currently works as an aviation safety consultant. He and his wife, Linda, live near Rideau Ferry, Ontario, Canada, and they have two sons. He is an avid outdoorsman and is training for his black belt in Karate. He is a member of the Manitoba Sports Hall of Fame.

ISBN 1553955565-X